Combating the Good Combat - How to Fight Terrorism with a Peacekeeping Mission

Rogerio Cietto

Published by Rogerio Cietto, 2012.

ABSTRACT

This work discusses the new challenge that terrorism imposes on the international community in the Twenty First century, the international actors in position to tackle it, the instruments available to counter them, and the methods to implement them. After a brief description of the three generations of peace operations carried on by the United Nations and other international and regional actors, we will expose the legal framework for international relations concerning the use of force, that are, International Humanitarian Law and Human Rights Law. Later, we will explain the threat to international peace and security that constitutes terrorism, its forms, methods and motivations, as well as its relations to peacekeeping. After, we will assume that terrorism should be considered a crime under international law, in order to punish their actors effectively. After a brief presentation of the UN System, and its organs related to peacekeeping and terrorism, we will discuss the efforts made so far to combat terror, especially the gathering of intelligence. In the end, we affirm the need to respect International Humanitarian Law and Human Rights, and also defend State Sovereignty, to fight terrorism in the long term. This research is based on an extensive research relying on an extended bibliography.

Keywords: Peace Operations. Terrorism. Human Rights. International Humanitarian Law.

RÉSUMÉ

Ce travail présente le nouveau défi que le terrorisme impose à la communauté internationale au XXIème siècle ainsi queles acteurs internationaux en mesure d'y faire face, les instruments disponibles pour les contrer, et les méthodes pour les mettre en œuvre. Après une brève description des trois générations des opérations de paix menées par les Nations Unies et par autres acteurs internationaux et régionaux, nous exposons le cadre juridique pour les relations internationales concernant l'usage de la force, quee sont le Droit internationale humanitaire et les Droits de l'homme. Plus tard, nous présenterons la menace à la paix et la sécurité internationales quee représente le terrorisme, ses formes, méthodes et motivations, ainsi que ses relations avec les opérations de paix. Par après, nous exposerons notre vision, à savoir que le terrorisme doit être considéré comme un crime de droit international, dans le but de punir ses acteurs de manière efficace. Après une présentation du système des Nations Unies, et ses organes dédiés à la paix et au terrorisme, nous discuterons des efforts déployés jusqu'ici pour lutter contre la terreur, en particulier les efforts liés à la collecte d'intelligence (au renseignement). Pour finaliser, nous réaffirmerons la nécessité de respecter le Droit international humanitaire et les Droits de l'homme, et aussi défendre la souveraineté de l' État, pour combattre le terrorisme sur le long terme. Notre recherche repose sur une bibliographie et une documentation exhaustive.

Mot-clés: Opérations de Paix. Terrorisme. Droits de l'Homme. Droit international humanitaire.

DEDICATORY

This study is offered, firstly, to God, who allowed the achievement of our goals and looked after for each and every detail. My sincere thanks to my family, Camila, Maísa and Alessa, for every moment I had to be absent, due to meetings and countless days in front of books and computers, and also for the daily support and help, which provided essential conditions for the accomplishment of this work.

Mes sincères remerciements pour M. Yvan Connoir, de lUQAM et du Peace Operations Training Institute (POTI), pour l'orientation et avis sur cette travail.

My thanks to Col Nolasco, Col Lamim and Col Napolis, from the Brazilian Battalion in Haiti, for all support, experiences and examples.

"The right of war, therefore, is derived from necessity and strict justice. If those who direct the conscience or councils of princes do not abide by this maxim, the consequence is dreadful: when they proceed on arbitrary principles of glory, convenience and utility, torrents of blood must overspread the earth" Charles de Secondat, Baron de Montesquieu, The Spirit of the Laws. Université de Nice, 2010.

TABLE OF ACRONYMS

AC *Ante Christum* (Latin)
COL Colonel
COTIPSO Certificate of Training in Peace Support Operations
CT Counter Terrorism
CTC Counter Terrorism Committee
CTED Counter Terrorism Executive Directorate
DPKO Department of Peacekeeping Operations
DDA Department for Disarmament Affairs
DPA Department of Political Affairs
ECOSOC Economic and Social Council
FBI Federal Bureau of Investigation
FCE *Forces Conventionnelles en Europe* (French)
GA General Assembly
ICC International Criminal Court
ICCPR International Covenant on Civil and Political Rights
ICJ International Court of Justice
ICTR International Criminal Tribunal for Rwanda
ICTY International Criminal Tribunal for the former Yugoslavia
IHL International Humanitarian Law
ISAF International Security Assistance Force
LoAC Law of Armed Conflict
MBA Master of Business Administration
MO Military Observers
MINUSTAH *Mission de Nations Unies pour la Stabilisation d'Haïti* (French)
NSA National Security Agency
OAS Organization of American States
OCHA Office for the Coordination of Humanitarian Affairs
ODCCP Office for Drug Control and Crime Prevention
ONUC Opération des Nations Unies au Congo

ONUCA *Observadores de las Naciones Unidas en Centroamerica* (Spanish)

Res Resolution

ROE Rules of Engagement

SALT Strategic Arms Limitation Talks

SC Security Council

SG Secretary General

START Strategic Arms Reduction Treaty

TC Trusteeship Council

TCC Troop Contributing Countries

TSP Terrorist Surveillance Program

UN United Nations

UNAVEM United Nations Verification Mission in Angola

UNIFIL United Nations Interim Force in Lebanon

UNIIMOG United Nations Iran-Iraq Military Observer Group

UNGOMAP United Nations Good Offices Mission in Afghanistan and Pakistan

UNMIK United Nations Mission in Kosovo

UNMIL United Nations Mission in Liberia

UNTAET United Nations Transitional Administration in East Timor

UNTSO United Nations Truce Supervision Organization in Palestine

USA United States of America

USSR Union of Soviet Socialist Republics

1. INTRODUCTION

During the time this paper was written, the War on Terror (Declared by George W. Bush in Sep, 12th , 2001, 10h53m Washington time, <news.bbc.co.uk>) carried out by some Western countries had made public what they called a major success in this mission: the death of Osama Bin Laden in Pakistan, leader of the organization called Al Qa'ida, and the dismantlement of his organization. Other factions supported by Al Qa'ida, like the Talebans in Afghanistan, are also said to be weakened and demoralized.

It seems contradictory that, after this so-called success in the War on Terror, initiated after the events occurred in September 11th, 2001, international peace and security are still threatened by retaliatory attacks of terrorist groups. Maybe this mission in Pakistan provided what terrorists need most: a martyr to mirror themselves, and ideals that, although corrupt, still motivate many to die and to kill.

Besides, the allegations of human rights violations of detainees accused or suspected of being involved with terrorism may fuel the hatred that terrorists need in order to recruit new members for their cause. For those who know only poverty and suffer for all their lives, believing in a fantastic world is easy, and all what the new recruits must do to pursue his terrorist mission is to believe that terror is the only way s/he can change his miserable condition.

Terrorism works by inculcating fear in a population, and as a result the government loses its credibility, because their citizens expect a certain level of security from the State they live. However, if the government itself acts in an aggressive way against its population, for the purpose of fighting criminals or terrorists, the government loses its credibility in the same manner. In both cases, the terrorist wins some deference from the population.

The objective of the present study is to show an alternative solution to the fight against terrorism, since the War on Terror, despite its achievements, needs to be readdressed in order to eliminate the causes that make a terrorist come into existence. By preventing the root causes of terror, the ideals and beliefs of terrorism will be weakened.

In order to show how terror can be fought on the long term, and be expelled from a specific population (minorities in a fragile country, for example), it is necessary to understand some important issues:

- Who has the authority to combat terrorism?

- What are the causes that proportionate terrorism to begin?

- What efforts have been made to fight terrorism?

- What is terrorism, what are the terrorists' objectives and motivations?

- What are the rules and laws that regulate this situation?

International terrorism, like any threat to international peace and security, is within the jurisdiction of the United Nations Security Council, which is responsible for authorizing, or not, measures against rogue countries or governments that stimulate or support terrorist activities, including the use of force, i. e., military activities, economic embargoes, arms embargoes, among others.

For the purpose of this study, we will present the different kinds of peace operations carried out by United Nations, for three reasons, which show the relation between terrorists, in one side, and Blue Helmets in another:

- Terrorism is more likely to raise and be sustained in fragile countries, with a weak sovereignty, because groups can maintain their activities without local repression;

Example: Al-Qa'ida terrorist training camps were made possible in Afghanistan only because the national government was not able to detect and stop its activities.

- Governments that do not respect, or do not care for the human rights of its population create also a good field for hiring new members for a terrorist cause.

Example: religious and ethnic intolerance and hatred between Tutsis and Hutus in Rwanda resulted in terrorist acts in which women and children were killed or mutilated (children which had their hands chopped by machetes in order to cause fear to the entire ethnic group).

- When the Government uses force arbitrarily to maintain its power among its population, some citizens may join rebel forces to protest, and this helps terrorists.

Example: the energic way the Haitian Political Police (*Les Tonton Macoutes*) dealt with the population during the government of Jean-Claude Duvalier (*Bébé Doc*) may make Haitians oppose the government, and give support to local gangs to struggle the State (this support is usually indirect, with food, fuel and hiding from the authorities).

Countries with these sorts of problems, in the past and nowadays, are of concern of the United Nations Security Council when they become a threat or breach to international peace and security, and some of them had, or still has, a Peace Operation deployed in its territory. Since they are used to this kind of operation, and are trained to deal with this situation, the Blue Helmets can be an alternative solution for the menace of terrorism, if properly authorized and employed.

In this study we will present the evolution of peace operations implemented by the United Nations, the principles and guidelines that guide their activities, its origins during the Cold War, their change of role and responsibility after the end of the Cold War, the reformulation of its objectives after a period of retrenchment, and its main successes and failures.

Later on, we will expose the main legal instruments that may be applicable in international relations among states and individuals, embodied in the rules of International Humanitarian Law, whose obligations should be respected by all actors involved, the Governments, the military, the other stakeholders and the UN personnel.

What terrorism is, how it was used by individuals and governments in different places of the world and during the human history and for what reason, what are the primary or secondary targets of terrorist acts, and where and how terrorism is more likely to flourish, will be explained in the sequence.

Then we will introduce the controversial discussion about the legal definition and jurisdictional competence for examining allegations of terrorism acts and prosecuting its actors, definition of high importance for the repression of this kind of crime, and necessary not to evade from the rule of law when taking coercive measures.

Conflicts of competence may arise when two or more jurisdictional organs believe they are the only responsible organ for proceeding criminal procedures against terrorists. These conflicts may happen between States, or between a State and an international court. The legal doctrine to solve this impasse is presented thereafter.

For a better comprehension of the UN System, we will also review the UN Charter, its objectives, its main organs and attributions, especially the Secretariat and the Security Council, their role and capacity in dealing with a peace operation and receives a report about acts of terrorism, in order to respond to it accordingly.

A brief study of the main Resolutions from the Security Council, Res 1373 (2001), 1456 (2003) and 1566 (2004) is made, in order to show the main efforts, and consequences, of the directions given in order to face the terrorist menace.

Finally, two main topics deserve attention concerning the War on Terror:

- Are the available instruments of International Humanitarian Law and Human Rights Law adequate to face the new challenges that terrorism presents? Are IHL a setback when fighting terror, or the, or a solution to fight terror properly?

- Is the Sovereignty of a State disrupted when another State, or a coalition of States, or the International Community, takes an action within its territory against terrorist groups? Is it possible that this action targets the State's Sovereignty, or shields it from local actors?

A reasonable answer to all these questions is necessary if the International Community wants to address long-term solutions to menaces against international peace and security. Certainly this study cannot provide all these solutions, but our objective is to bring new ideas, methods and procedures to the attempt of solving a problem that is known to exist throughout history, and is far from ended.

The title of this paper was inspired in the letter of Saint Paul to Timothy, 4, 7 ("*I fought the good fight. I finished the race* (also translated as *career* in some languages). *I kept the faith.*"). Since the translation of the Bible has some differences in every language, it is used the expression "combating the good combat" instead of "fighting the good fight" because the version of the Bible in Portuguese uses the verb "to combat", and this verb is more related to armed conflicts.

2. HISTORY OF PEACE OPERATIONS

Before the UN Charter, some efforts were made in order to prevent a conflict to arise, mainly by regional actors. Some examples are the Delian League of Ancient Greece in the Fifth Century AC, the *Pax Dei* (Peace of God) and *Treuga Dei* (Truce of God), by the medieval Catholic Church, prohibiting all kinds of hostilities in certain occasions (from the first Sunday of the Advent to the Epiphany, or from Wednesday afternoon to Sunday morning, in memory of the Resurrection of Jesus Christ).

Later on, Emeric Crucé offered, in 1623, an option for conflict prevention. His idea was that all state leaders, within Europe or not, should make an alliance in order to settle international disputes through mediation at a world council held in a neutral location. This idea was followed by other peace-oriented agreements like the Peace of Westphalia (1648), Utretch (1713), and Paris (1763).

The first system that attempted to deal thoroughly with conflict prevention was the League of Nations, created after the First World War, with the mission of regulating the use of force in the disputes between States, using collective diplomacy and peace enforcement. Unfortunately, it could not stop World War II, so the United Nations were created, in 1945, not to regulate war, but to prevent an armed conflict, *ipsis litteris, "to prevent future generations from the scourge of war"* (Preamble of the UN Charter).

According to the UN Charter (Art. 1), war is not a licit mean of conflict resolution, and any dispute shall be solved by pacific means, according to the principles of International law. The use of force is a prerogative of the Security Council (Chapter VII), against acts threatening international peace and security, and only when other measures will have been made ineffective, like the interruption of diplomatic relations or an economic embargo. The use of force is also possible in cases of legitimate defense, against an armed aggression (Art. 51).

There's no legal provision for Peace Operations in the UN Charter. The Security Council may decide that there is a breach of international peace and security and, using the powers of Chapter VI (Pacific Settlement of Disputes) and Chapter VII (Acts in cases of Threat to Peace, Breach of Peace and Acts of Aggression) of the Charter, drafts a Resolution with a specific mandate, using military forces with the objective to preserve peace between warring parties.

Due to the disagreement between the two superpowers of the Security Council (USA and USSR during the Cold War, Peace Operations were created as a solution for conflict resolution, a resort to other means to preserve peace and stability. They began as unarmed observers of ceasefires between States, and later included troops from different countries, and the use of force was legal only in self-defense. Ultimately, Peace Operations include efforts to reconstruct the political institutions and the Rule of Law of a given country.

Peace Operations are not an exclusivity of the UN System, although the majority of the soldiers deployed today use the UN Blue Helmet and distinctive UN signs on their fatigues. Regional Organizations, based on the dispositions of Chapter VIII of the Charter, and authorized by the Security Council, may use troops to prevent threats or menaces to peace and security. For example, we could recall the Inter American Peace Force, created in 1965 by the Organization of American States (OAS) and deployed in the Dominican Republic to prevent violence to arise due to the political instability following the assassination of the dictator Rafael Trujillo in 1961.

UN Peace Operation's history may be distinguished in three different periods: during the Cold War (1948 to 1987), following the

Cold War (1988 to 1996), and the resurgence of Peace Operations (1996 to today).

2.1. PEACE OPERATIONS DURING THE COLD WAR

Military observers (MO's) were used for the first time in 1947, during hostilities in Indonesia, to supervise a ceasefire signed between the Royal Dutch Army and the Indonesian Government, and assist in the repatriation of Dutch forces. It used the powers of Chapter VI of the Charter, mainly diplomacy.

The Security Council took a decision against a breach of the peace during the Korean Crisis, in 1950. However, it was not a Peace Operation, because the forces were not under the direction of the Secretary-General, or the Security Council.

The first Peace Operation was created to face the Arab-Israeli Crisis, in 1948, after the creation of the state of Israel. United Nations Truce Supervision Organization in Palestine (UNTSO), which is working until today, has the mission to monitor if the truce is observed by the warring factions. The name "peacekeeping" wasn't mentioned, but it was the first time that military observers were deployed after a conflict.

The principles of impartiality and consent were defined by Ralph Bunche, among other principles that guide the organization and functioning of UNTSO. He also decided that military observers should not carry any kind of weapons, in order to prevent an engagement against them by any party.

The controversy about the nationality of the military observers was resolved by requesting personnel to all members of the Truce Commission. They remained linked to their respective national army for administrative purposes, but received orders from UN authorities, and received their national payment plus an UN allowance. They wore an UN armband over their national uniforms.

With the help of UNTSO mediators, Israel signed armistices with four Arab States (Egypt, Jordan, Lebanon and Syria). The Security Council gave autonomy to UNTSO and placed it under the authority of the Secretary-General, becoming the first peacekeeping operation in UN history.

It is expected from the host countries (that receive the UN troops on their soil) a high degree of cooperation with the UN staff, and assurance for of their safety, according to the Conventions of Immunities and Privileges of the United Nations.

The peacekeepers have the competence to deal with complaints concerning the ceasefire made by local civilians or the separated parties. Monitoring a ceasefire means report any act that may be interpreted as hostile towards one of the parties, for example:
- Presence of troops or equipment in demilitarized zones;
- Presence of defensive areas in demilitarized zones;
- Shooting across a demarcation line between the parties;
- Over-flights on prohibited airspace;
- Unauthorized crossing of the demarcation line.

Other UN Observation Missions were deployed at the India-Pakistan border in 1949 and also 1969, Lebanon in 1958, Yemen in 1963, Dominican Republic in 1965. All of them had straightforward tasks, like monitoring a border area, supervising the retracting of troops or a ceasefire or an armistice, and usually with a limited duration.

2.2. PEACE OPERATIONS FOLLOWING THE COLD WAR

The rivalry between the two superpowers began to diminish after the withdrawal of Soviet troops from Afghanistan, and the consequences of the arms race with the USA to the Russian economy. The new policy implemented by Mikhail Gorbatchev, called *Glasnost* (Political openness) and *Perestroika* (Economic restructuring) decreased international tensions, and the relations between Soviet Union, later Russia, and the USA changed, from competition to cooperation.

After the Cold War, new peacekeeping missions were deployed, with the support of the two superpowers, and accomplished their missions:

- UN Good Offices Mission in Afghanistan and Pakistan (UNGOMAP) in 1988, to monitor the withdrawal of Soviet troops, and receive complaints concerning violations of the ceasefire;

- UN Iran-Iraq Military Observer Group (UNIIMOG) in 1987, to establish and monitor ceasefire lines, and supervise the withdrawal of forces;

- UN Angola Verification Mission (UNAVEM) in 1988, to monitor the withdrawal of Cuban forces from Angola, and supervise the peace process carried on by warring parties;

- UN Observer Group in Central America, in Costa Rica, El Salvador, Guatemala, Honduras and Nicaragua (ONUCA) in 1989, whose complex mission was to observe the compliance of the governments in stopping supporting irregular forces and insurrectionist movements (including the use of facilities of radio and television broadcast for military operations), and to not attack one State through the territory of another state;

- UN Transition Assistance Group, in Namibia, to supervise the ceasefire with South Africa, to monitor the retracting of South African troops, as well as rebel movements.

Other Missions during the 1988-1996 period were considered a failure (RAM, Sunil. The History of United Nations Peacekeeping Operations *following the Cold War*, pg. 219), because of:

- Passivity in Bosnia, due to the lack of commitment in restructuring the local police, the judicial system, and the maintenance of law and order;

- Lack of efficiency in Haiti, because UNMIH was not able to qualify the Haitian National Police and promote national reconciliation and economic rehabilitation;

- Insensitivity in Rwanda, because it didn't react in time to prevent the genocide;

- Too much agressivity and lack of commitment in Somalia, because international humanitarian relief agencies were robbed by militias and armed bandits.

Other reasons for the failure of some peacekeeping missions is the change in the nature of the conflict, from the Inter-State conflicts characterized by the dispute between the two superpowers and their allies, to intra-State conflicts, with many local armed factions, irregular forces and militias, who respect ceasefires only when it gave them a military advantage.

After some setbacks, Secretary-General Boutros Boutros-Ghali concluded his Supplement to *An Agenda for Peace* (Idem, pg. 180), in January 1995, reiterating the need of a strict adherence to the principles of consent, impartiality and minimum use of force, and warned of the danger of deceiving the distinction between peacekeeping and peace enforcement. The latter should be delegated by a major power or a regional organization.

Also, the cornerstone principles of peacekeeping have been interpreted, in order to be used in a more pragmatic way:

- Consent shall be given at the strategic level (by the state authority) rather than the tactical level (by the population);

- Impartiality (not taking sides in a conflict) is different than Neutrality (not interfere in the internal affairs of a country);

- The UN shall be prepared to defend civilians, even if the mandate is not explicit about this power, because such mission is expected by the presence of UN troops.

2.3. RESURGENCE OF PEACE OPERATIONS

The failures of some peacekeeping missions during the period 1988 – 1996 led to major changes on the size, scope and complexity of this kind of UN instrument. Multidimensional objectives were included, so the Blue Helmets are to have skills in human rights, civil policing, electoral assistance, refugee relief, and nation-building abilities, Basic military skills are still necessary, but it is not enough.

The missions of alleviating human suffering and create institutions to build a self-sustaining peace are the same, but the methodology has changed.

These multidimensional peacekeeping missions consist of a military component, that is armed, but eventually it may not use weapons, and a civilian component for the nation-building tasks. The basic objectives of these new peace operations are to:

- Prevent a conflict before it begins, or impede it to cross the borders of the country;

- Monitor a ceasefire and stabilize a conflict situation, in order to create conditions for a lasting peace agreement;

- Help in the implementation of comprehensive peace agreements;

- Assist States in the transition to a government based on democracy, good governance and economic development.

The resurgence started after the Brahimi Report (RAM, Sunil. *The History of United Nations Peacekeeping Operations from Retrenchment to Resurgence*, pg. 131), in August 2000. It recommended restructuring the Department of Peacekeeping Operations (DPKO), an analysis unit to assist in information concerning peace and security to all UN departments, and an integrated task force in New York to plan and support a peace operation from its birth.

The Brahimi Report also listed some conditions for a successful peace operation:

- Create strategies to prevent conflicts;
- Have a clear and specific mandate;
- Rules of engagement adequate to the situation;
- The parties to the conflict agree to the operation;
- Adequate human resources, as well as equipment and financial support;
- When the UN is given temporary executive powers, an interim criminal code;
- Traditional peacekeeping should be deployed within 30 days;
- For complex peacekeeping, the deployment should occur within 90 days.

As a result of the Brahimi Report, since 2006 the DPKO has a situation centre, which works 24 hours a day, 7 days a week, and a Military Division was created and well staffed. Also, the DPKO has been staffed with more military and police advisers, and the UNHQ has more personnel to support peace operation.

In a fragile State, rebuilding national capacities take time. However, Member States want quick solutions, and Troop Contributing Countries want to see their troops back home as fast as possible. This is the dichotomy that Peace Operations face today.

In the 1990's decade, UN troops were mainly sent by developed countries. However, after September 11th, 2001, many troop contributing countries shifted their resources (human, equipment and funds) to the War on Terror. Thus, the industrialized countries gave space for the developing nations to share an increased contribution to international peace and security.

Instead of a problem, this responsibility gave more fuel to peacekeeping missions, concerning the funding capability and the credibility of the mission, as follows:

- The exchange rate for the developing countries is favorable for UN payments. Since the UN pays in US dollars, the TCC sees this money multiplied when it is converted to its internal currency. The UN pays the same, but the country has more funds available.

- Developed countries are sometimes accused of imperialism, and of interfering in the internal issues of other countries for their benefit. So, the population may see UN troops as intruders. On the other hand, developing countries have, or had in their recent history, the same institutional problems the population of the host country is suffering. It makes a natural empathy between the UN troops and the population concerned, because the UN soldier, in this case, has seen this unfortunate scenario in his home country, and knows how to deal with it.

In brief, peace operations were created to deal with tensions between states, and were also successfully used in internal conflicts within feeble states, in an effort to mediate a solution, implement the dialogue between warring parties and protecting the civilian population. These field experiences are closely linked with the counterterrorism effort studied in this paper, and will be resumed further.

3. INTERNATIONAL HUMANITARIAN LAW AND HUMAN RIGHTS LAW

The international legal framework in which the Peace Operations work, mainly International Humanitarian Law, needs attentive study in order to understand the modern challenges that Terrorism, and the War on Terror, are imposing on it.

Each civilization has created "humanity clusters", making a set or rules to limit the use of violence and also encouraging solidarity to the victims of a conflict. Often these rules were only applicable to the same members of the group or civilization. For example, Plato wrote that certain limitations must be observed in the wars between Greek cities, but these limits were not applicable to the fight against the Persians (VEUTHEY, Michel. *Droit International Humanitaire*).

These rules were intended to guarantee the survival of the population. Warriors should not attack women and children, destroy crop fields or trees, poison water sources or destroy sacred places and buildings, because these actions might endanger the survival of the population.

The simplest and plus common definition of IHL is the "Golden Rule", defined as *Do not do to others what you don't want others do to you*. This demand of reciprocity in the limitation on the use of force and in solidarity concerning humanitarian action is present in most religious traditions, like Hinduism, Confucianism, Shintoism, Buddhism, Taoism, Zoroastrianism, Judaism, Christianism and Islamism.

In Asian countries, Buddhism, Hinduism and also Taoism, Confucionism and Shintoism, list principles of Humanity for the treatment of the enemy during an Armed Conflict. Example: Japanese *Bushido* (*Bushi* = Samurai, and *Do* = Way).

Buddhism has two fundamental principles: *maitri* (benevolence) and *karuna* (mercy, compassion), very close to the meaning of humanity (MILLET-DEVALLE, Anne-Sophie. *Religions et Droit International Humanitaire*).

Hinduism has rules about the humane treatment of defeated enemies, as well as loyalty in combat, and the use of weapons that cause superfluous injury. The Laws of Manou (a code of laws with moral and religious norms) prescribe that a warrior must never use against its enemies treacherous weapons like sticks with blades, poisoned arrows or leather in fire (MILLET-DEVALLE, Anne-Sophie. *Religions et Droit International Humanitaire*).

Manou Laws also prohibit to attack an enemy: on foot (when the attacker is in a vehicle), who acts femininely, that joins his hands begging for mercy, scalped, seated, or sleeping, or is not wearing armor, completely naked, disarmed, observing the combat or fighting with another enemy, or whose weapon is broken, or laid on the floor, or seriously injured, or a coward or when he is running away.

Two Indian sacred books, *Ramayana* and *Mahabhata*, forbid the use of weapons of mass destruction, which do not permit to distinguish combatants from non-combatants. In *Mahabharata*, "Arjuna (religious Indian character), abiding to the laws of war, abstained from using *pasupathastra*, an hyper destructive weapon, because the combat demanded ordinary classical weapons only, so the use of extraordinary or non classic weapons would be not only contrary to the religion or the known laws of war, but also immoral." (*Apud* BALMOND, Louis. *Droit du recours à la force*).

Judge Weeramantry, from the International Court of Justice (ICJ) used this passage as an argument in his dissident opinion about the Consultative Advice of ICJ about the legality of the Threat or the Use of Nuclear Weapons, arguing that the Court shall guarantee, in its whole, the representation of the different forms of civilization and the main legal systems in the world.

The judge also quoted the passage in Deuteronomy (fifth book of the Pentateuch, Old Testament) that prohibited the chop of fruit trees (Deuteronomy 20, 19 "When you lay siege to a city for a long time, in making war against it to take it, you shall not destroy the trees thereof by forcing an axe against them : for you may eat of them, and you shall not cut them down (for the trees of the field is man's life), to employ them in the siege"), the African tribal habits, the prohibition of the weapon called crossbow by the Latran Council of 1139, as well as the very well detailed doctrine of Saint Thomas Aquinas, about, among other subjects, the protection of non-combatants.

The Western Christianity tried to create limits through the traditions of Cavalry and proclaim, in Centuries X and XI, the *Treuga Dei* (Truce of God) and *Pax Dei* (Peace of God), an initiative of the church. According to these proclaims, it was prohibited all hostilities in certain periods of the liturgical calendar (from the first Sunday of the Advent to the Epiphany, from Ash Wednesday to the Ascension) and in certain days of the week (from Wednesday afternoon to Sunday morning, in memory of the Passion and Resurrection of Jesus Christ).

The first defenders of International Humanitarian Law, not by coincidence, were religious, that recognized the inherent dignity of every human being, created by the image of God, as Saint Thomas Aquinas (1225 a 1274), the Dominican Francisco de Vitoria (1483-1546), Baltazar Ayala (1548-1584), the jesuit Francisco Suarez (1548-1617) and the Swiss protestant Emmerich de Vattel (1714-1767).

The codification of the Law of Armed Conflict (LoAC) has begun by the initiative of Tzar Alexander II, of Russia, where delegates of 15 European States held a meeting in Brussels in July 27th, 1874, to study the project of an international agreement about the laws and practices of war. The initial text was adopted with a few changes. However, many States hadn't wanted to accept a mandatory agreement, so this text wasn't ratified. Anyway, this was the first important step for the codification of the Laws of War (VEUTHEY, Michel. *Droit International Humanitaire*).

The Institute of International Law, during a session in Geneva, nominated a Committee to examine the Declaration of Brussels and submit to the Institute its opinion and complementary propositions. The efforts of the Institute led to the adoption, in 1880, of the Oxford Manual about the Law of Land Warfare. The Declaration of Brussels and the Oxford Manual was the base for two Hague Conventions, concerning land warfare and related dispositions, adopted in 1899 and 1907.

Over the centuries, many nations started to have the conviction that Law must impose itself in the sphere of conflicts, in order to limit its most disastrous effects. The development of new ways of communication, of weapons of mass destruction and weaponry even more sophisticated had led to a world consciousness about inhumane and sanguinolent characteristics of contemporaneous conflicts.

This consciousness had a notorious evolution from the XIX Century, with the practice of coalitions, capitulations and armistice conventions. These evolutions, aimed to humanize the treatment of the victims of the conflict, were born from consuetudinary rules, revealing the development of some combating ethics.

A valid process of construction of international legal norms has started during the second half of the XIX Century, with the efforts of Henri Dunant in Europe, who witnessed the cruel battle of Solferino, and after idealized the First Geneva Convention, in 1864, and Francis Lieber, who wrote the first promulgated code about this subject, by the government of the United States of America during the Secession Civil War.

During the XX Century, this evolution took place with the Geneva Conventions in 1906 and Hague Conventions in 1899 and 1907. By codifying a legal framework that was at the time part of international consuetudinary law, these Conventions show the beginning of a humanitarian law to protect victims and a law concerning war, to limit the combatant's actions.

The International Humanitarian Law and the Law of War evolved and were granted some efficiency, but First World War has shown, for the first time, the incomplete characteristic of these norms, and the difficulties for its implementation by States. New conventional tools tried to fill the lacunes of a legal framework that does not protect satisfactorily. Second World War, on its turn, put in evidence the need for a complete set of rules that guarantee the protection of the victims of war more efficiently. This was the contribution of the Four Geneva Conventions, at August 12th, 1949, which constitute nowadays the foundation of Humanitarian Law. These Conventions were highlighted in the trials of Nuremberg and Tokyo, where for the first time accused of war crimes were condemned.

During the second half of the XXth Century there was an increase in the field of applicability of the LoAC, inside an international community whose functioning is based on the Charter of the United Nations. The LoAC contains aspects from the protection of cultural properties, natural environment, the participation of children in armed conflicts, or the prohibition of certain weapons, considered inhumane or that cause excessive suffer.

In parallel, the physiognomy of the armed conflict was largely modified. Internal conflicts brought new non-State actors (like terrorist organizations), creating multiple international repercussions, and at the same time peacekeeping and peace enforcement operations are even more common after the end of the Cold War.

The International Law of Armed Conflict is a specific branch of Public International Law, and has three different domains.

The Law of War, also known as the "Hague Law", regroups the normative framework of the Hague Conventions, from whom the most known are those promulgated at October 18th, 1907; one is about the law and practices of land warfare, and another about naval warfare. These texts are designed to protect the combatant from the most horrible effects of war, and they define some rules applicable to combat, like the prohibition of perfidy or to declare that there will be no prisoners (give no quarter). The rules derived from them are intended to protect certain rights that are also threatened, like the Hague Convention at May 14th, 1954, concerning the protection of cultural properties.

International Humanitarian Law encompasses the framework made by the Geneva Conventions of August 12th, 1949, about the Wounded and sick (First), the Shipwrecked (Second), the Prisoners of War (Third) and the Civil population (Fourth). These Four Conventions are intended to protect the victims of war, in other words, the combatants *hors de combat* and the civilian population that suffers from the horrid effects of conflicts. From the beginning of the XXth Century, the proportion of civilian victims of wars is much higher than military victims.

In the division between the Law of War and Humanitarian Law there is a combined law, which includes elements of both branches. They are the two Additional Protocols to the Geneva Conventions, adopted in June 8th, 1977, in Geneva.

The Law of Arms Control gathers the international conventions that prohibit, limit or regulate the use of certain weapons and ammunitions. It prohibits chemical and biological weapons, anti-personal mines, hollow-point projects ("dum dum" bullets), weapons with projectiles not detectable by X-rays, blinding lasers, among others. The use of incendiary weapons, for its turn, is regulated and limited to the exclusive attack of military objectives away from a civilian concentration. In the same manner, the use of mines that are not anti-personal is still authorized, but only if all precautions are taken to protect civilians from its effects, including after the conflict.

The Law of Arms Control completes the international instruments concerning disarmament, like the Nuclear Weapons Non-Proliferation Treaty, treaty FCE (*Forces Conventionnelles en Europe*) or START (*Strategic Arms Reduction Treaty*) and SALT (*Strategic Arms Limitations Talks*). These instruments are parallel to the Arms Control, for they both aim a progressive reduction of certain weapons, until its total disappearance, because the subject Arms Control is more than the prohibition of certain weapons.

It is during an Armed Conflict that the sovereign power of a State manifests mostly its strength. In this meaning, some States do not hesitate to privilege military efficiency in detriment to legal rules. On the contrary, the respect of the Law of Armed Conflict permits the execution of military operations, limiting the inhumane effects of war. This is an essential condition for avoiding the occurrence of the vicious circle of barbarism.

The framework of the Law of Armed Conflict, although imperfect, constitutes a valuable protection, for the Armed Forces and also for the civilian population. They allow the solution, or the attempt for a solution, of situations that are difficult, complex or ambiguous, which characterize all armed conflicts. They delimit the action of the Armed Forces, contributing for the country's image in the occasion of an external intervention.

The Law of Armed Conflict is applicable to every armed conflict. This may be international, when it occurs between two sovereign States, or non-international, whose plus frequent example is the civil war. Non-International Armed Conflicts must be differentiated from situations of Internal Tension, insurrections and other analogous acts of violence, which are not considered conflicts.

Such distinction is important because from it derives the legal framework that is applicable to each circumstance. Thus, concerning International Humanitarian Law, a Non-International Armed Conflict is regulated by Additional Protocol II to the Geneva Conventions. On the other side, in an International Armed Conflict the warring parties must comply with the Four Geneva Conventions and Additional Protocol I. The applicable rules to International Armed Conflicts are broader and more protective than Non-International Armed Conflicts.

The core of the fundamental rights of the human being is applicable to every situation, even outside a conflict, and independent of its character, international or not. It is the 3rd common article to the Geneva Conventions, which define the basic rules for the protection of the human being, and also the legal framework of Human Rights, that list three important principles:

- **Inviolability**, that guarantees to every person and every combatant the right for the respect of his life and his physical and moral integrity;

- **Non discrimination**, so every person is treated without distinction of race, gender, nationality, political opinion or religion (this principle of Human Rights is different than the Principle of Discrimination, specific for International Humanitarian Law, explained below);

- **Certainty**, so the individual is not held responsible for something he/she did not commit, through the needed judicial guarantees and the prohibition of reprisals, collective punishments, hostage taking and deportations.

The rules of International Humanitarian Law are aimed to protect the combatants in an armed conflict, but also the sick, wounded, shipwrecked, health and religious personnel, prisoners of war, war correspondents, diplomats, humanitarian organizations and civil protection agents, refugees and, as a whole, the civilian population affected by a situation of an armed conflict, especially women and children.

The main principles of International Humanitarian Law are:

- **Humanity**, that lies in the desire to avoid, through all available measures, superfluous damage and suffer caused by the use of force. In this way, the choice of methods and means of warfare is not unlimited, but it must respect LoAC rules that limit the pernicious effects of the use of violence. The Martens Clause (This Clause has been created by the Estonian jurist Frédéric de Martens, and is part of a number of international conventions) disposes that: "The civilian population and the combatant remain under the protection of the *Droit des Gens* (*Jus gentium*, or International Law), the rules resulted from established customs, the principles of humanity and the requirements of public consciousness". The respect to the Law of Armed Conflict follows a logic of humanity. Every battle won with disrespect to human dignity is, sooner or later, a lost fight;

- **Discrimination**, also known as Principle of Precaution, imposes to combatants the obligation to distinguish military objectives, which may be attacked, from the civilian population and properties, which may not be the target of any voluntary attack. One of the greatest difficulties when implementing this principle is to find a practical form of distinction between military objectives and civilian properties. Art. 52 of Additional Protocol I to the Geneva Conventions clarifies: "concerning properties, military objectives are limited to those which for its nature, location, destination or utilization, show an effective military contribution to the military action, and its total or partial destruction, capture or neutralization bring a concrete military advantage";

- **Proportionality**, requiring the abstention of an attack in which one can predict that it will cause incidentally losses of human life in the civilian population, wounds to the civilian population, damage to civilian properties, or a group of losses and damage, considered excessive in comparison to the concrete military advantage that is directly expected. The implementation of this principle lies in the adequacy between the means employed and the aimed military result. The execution of the Principle of Proportionality does not exclude the collateral damage that may affect the civilian population or properties, unless they are exaggerated in comparison to the concrete military advantage that is directly expected. Neither does it excludes that some objectives, benefiting from a special protection from an international convention, become military targets, if this convention explicitly mentions the faculty for the attacker to argue the existence of a military necessity to inflict the attack.

Respecting LoAC is a guarantee of efficacy in the accomplishment of the mission. It improves the behavior of the combatant, invigorating the feeling of discipline. It also eases the management and conclusion of a crisis, and the return to peace, in a moment when all these questions are primordial in every intervention abroad.

In the equilibrium between the Principle of Humanity and Military Necessities, the LoAC is in the azimuth of the Principle of Economy of Forces and Means.

In order to be efficient, the LoAC must be respected by the great majority of States, if not all. It must find universality, so it may be accepted by everyone. It must also be rounded by measures of trust, supervision, control and sanction.

In the same way that obligations born from individual and collective morality are implemented voluntarily, and not imposed in a random way, obligations born from Law gather the population of a State that is trying to respect them, and they may be subject, if there's legal basis, of disciplinary and legal sanctions.

Combatants must respect, in any circumstance, the norms of LoAC. It is not acceptable, in any case, that the deviation of conduct away from them, independent of the context or the mission, even if the adversary does not respect them.

The Commander takes a comprehensive responsibility in this issue, and must assure that the members of the Armed Forces know the subject and implement the obligations that come from it. He is the responsible for the instruction and training of LoAC.

It is a misunderstanding from the Commander to believe that LoAC can be disregarded in the hypothesis that it diminishes military efficiency. There is no such hypothesis, and the reason is simple: when respecting LoAC, the troops become even more efficient, because:

- The shooting that hits non military targets generate an unnecessary waste of means and time in the battlefield, and the demoralization of the troops;

- The support of the civilian population is essential for the solution of any asymmetric conflict, restoring peace in the long term (primordial for Peace Operations);

- The respect for the natural environment helps to the reconstruction of the country in the post-conflict, facilitating the end of the conflict and the disengagement of troops in the field.

In addition to disciplinary measures that may be imposed, the inobservance of the LoAC norms may also conduct to criminal responsibility. The accused may be prosecuted for crimes in federal or military courts, or in international criminal courts, depending on the gravity and extension of the facts.

In conclusion, the soldier, Blue Helmet or not, who wants to understand and use the Law of Armed Conflict during his Mission must follow three basic procedures:

- Trust, because the rules of LoAC support the whole of the military doctrine and are considered in all ranks of hierarchy. The equilibrated development of these rules and its implementation constitute important objectives for countries that respect their international commitments. Also, the high standard behavior of the Peacekeepers may serve as an example for others combatants to learn and apply the same rules and standards;

- Reality, because the respect of the Law of Armed Conflict and the Human Rights Law are among the concerns of disciplined and organized Armed Forces. Even when some norms may seem complex or contradictory, its implementation lies in the respect of values that are important to democratic States, and which they are trying to protect. This implementation is based on the honesty and good faith that guide the Blue Helmet in the accomplishment of his mission;

- Perseverance, because the Law of Armed Conflict is not just a theoretical knowledge, but must become a state of mind that encourages the military institutions and each of its members, in all occasions. A permanent commitment at the strategic level makes that, in all subordinate levels, the soldier realizes that, by knowing and respecting the norms of Armed Conflicts, he is fulfilling his duties.

4. TERRORISM, OLD AND NEW FORMS

The word terror comes from the Latin word *terrere*, which means to scare. The word and its related terms were used in very different contexts – in the name of a tyrant (for example, Ivan the Terrible, the first Russian Tzar), or periods characterized by violent political instability (for example, the Reign of Terror during the French Revolution), and in sporadic acts of violence known worldwide as international terrorism. The violence is not the main aspect, because violence was committed during the First and the Second World War, and was not at this time considered as terrorism. The violence is not the objective, but the instrument by which one may spread fear (terrorize) in the population of a country.

Spreading fear may be driven by a criminal or political purpose. One way or another, the entire population may become frightened without the use of terrorism. For example, when the cause is a disease, like the Bird Flu from China, that threatened the whole world, or the Mad Cow Disease from France, which frightened even vegetarians, and also the deathly virus Ebola, which caused an epidemy in Central Africa during the 90's and beginning of the XXth Century. Some people believe that these sicknesses were not entirely natural, but were disseminated, characterizing a case of bioterrorism.

If one assumes that the intention of all terrorist is to widely disseminate fear in the population, there is a common motivation in the criminal offenses they commit. Since there is a common element in terrorism, countering it may be done using common defensive strategies and tactics. Any action that can be taken to reduce fear and anxiety in the population is an efficient counterterrorism tool.

4.1. DEFINITIONS OF TERRORISM

Brian Jenkins defines terrorism as the use or threat of the use of force with the objective of political change. Similarly, FBI defines terrorism as the illegal use of force or violence against people or property to intimidate or coerce a government, the civilian population, or a part of it, with social and political objectives (COUNTERTERRORISM, 2002, p. 16).

The International Convention for the Suppression of the Financing of Terrorism (Adopted by the UN General Assembly Resolution 54/109, of 9 December 1999), define terrorism as "criminal acts, including against civilians, committed with the intent to cause death or serious body injury, or taking of hostages, with the purpose to provoke a state of terror in the general public or in a group of persons or particular persons, intimidate a population or compel a government or an international organization, to do or to abstain from doing any act" We find a similar definition in Security Council Resolution 1566 (2004), adopted on 8 October 2004.

In conventional combat, or guerilla/asymmetrical combat, it is possible to distinguish combatants and non-combatants. One may argue that people not involved in combat are also killed during the conflict. In this case they are not the main target of the military action, but a side effect of the attack, called collateral damage. In conventional or guerilla warfare, the objective is to destroy the enemy forces. Armed conflicts may have high or low intensity (that is, occupying or not foreign territory), like many conflicts around the globe, about independence (ex-Soviet Union republics and ex-European colonies), ethnical minorities (in Africa and Oceania) and drug trafficking (Latin America). Armed conflicts may be symmetric (between States) and asymmetric (between a State and rebel groups or factions).

However, targeting non-combatants (through suffer and death) is the core of international terrorism. Due to the secret in which the activity is carried on, the terrorist act is done by a small group of agents, who receive logistical and financial support from fundamentalist organizations and sympathizing governments. Certain groups may be suspect of supporting terrorist objectives, when they are not doing the terror themselves. Distinction must be made between groups that are really the threat, from others that are explored or used as decoy by other groups.

The American Department of State describes terrorism as a phenomenon in constant change, and the nature of the terrorist threat changed dramatically. It attributed these changes to five factors (COUNTERTERRORISM, 2002, p. 26):

1. The collapse of the Soviet Union (and the end of the Warsaw Pact);

2. Change in the terrorist's motivation;

3. Proliferation of mass destruction technologies;

4. Increase in the access to information and information technology;

5. Accelerated centralization of essential components in national infrastructure, which increased the vulnerability to a terrorist attack.

4.2. INTENTION OF TERRORISM

Terrorism is usually a dramatization for political reasons (the specific intent of the terrorist attack, or *dolus specialis*, is explained in the next Chapter), and there are some universal elements in modern terrorist activities (COUNTERTERRORISM, 2002, p. 31 et all):

1. THE USE OF VIOLENCE TO PERSUADE, in which explosives and other attacks are used to gain positions with the victims-targets. The term Victims-targets is used because the objective is not the people who are hurt or killed. On the contrary, the attack may be executed to influence a government, a coalition or group of governments, in order to take a decision or a certain action, or also to prevent or repress a decision or action;

2. TARGETS AND VICTIMS CHOSEN FOR THE MAXIMUM OF PROPAGANDA ACHIEVABLE, so they choose targets that will provide the largest attention of the media. This fact is particularly outstanding by terrorist attacks like the explosion in World Trade Center in New York City in 1993 and 2001 and the taking of hostages with Israeli athletes during the Olympic Games in Munich in 1972. Other examples are the terrorist attacks in Madrid (March 11, 2004) and in London (July 7 2005);

3. ATTACKS ARE NOT PROVOKED, i. e., the victims or targets did nothing against the terrorists, which is true for any terrorist attack, since their alleged reasons are often a complex story that terrorists give to themselves to find support for their acts among their group;

4. MAXIMUM PUBLICITY WITH MINIMAL RISK is the leading principle of many terrorist actions, particularly those with explosives. Attacks with explosives usually create a good amount of publicity, depending on the location and the period, thus targets are selected for what they represent, like embassies, touristic attractions known worldwide, and similar facilities. High-technology timers to

allow the detonation to be planned to have a long delay, reducing the risk for the terrorist or terrorists, that may be far away when the devices explode or are found. Other favorite terrorist activities are kidnapping, robberies and assassinations, which may generate great and prolonged publicity, but also a higher risk for the agent. There is a tendency of a cyclical change in terrorist attacks. After a lot of kidnappings, the population may become insensible to the acts, and further hostage taking may not have the same attention of the media, from television news to the Internet. Attacks with explosives, being less frequent during the same period, may also gain more publicity than another kidnapping. Thus, a change of tactics may achieve more propaganda than other forms of attacks. Terrorists always want to have media coverage, so they will change tactics in order to have as much publicity as possible.

5. USE OF SURPRISE TO AVOID COUNTERTERRORIST MEASURES in order to attack high-protected targets. Even when there are guards, detection devices, and a high security in the surroundings, the surprise factor may be used to sidetrack the equipment and the human element in the security system. Time is the best friend of the terrorist. After a long time without any terrorist events, well-protected targets may have a decrease in the security measures. When there is no planning for a suicide attack, the terrorist will stay low until the security of the target is more favorable.

6. THREATS, CONSTRAINTS AND VIOLENCE are tools used by terrorist to maintain an environment of fear. Terrorist may plant small explosives or incendiary devices in public places, like department stores and movie theaters. Recently, terrorists who fight against the Egyptian government attacked tourists in the Pyramids and other historical sites. For the population, there is no link or reasonable connection between the motivation and the location of the attacks, so any threat of such activity may create fear among the population.

7. INDIFFERENCE FOR WOMEN AND CHILDREN AS VICTIMS, because sometimes places are specially chosen to make innocent victims, in order to increase the outrage and fear about the aggressivity of the terrorist act. This is also another way to receive more publicity and media coverage due to suffer and death of non-combatants. This peculiarity differentiates the terrorist and the soldier or the guerrillero. The soldier fights backed by the authority of his government. A guerrillero fights the same combat as the soldier in tactics and code of conduct, so women and children are not desired targets. A terrorist may possibly focus on women and children as targets, to instill a bigger feeling of fear. Therefore, the ethnic cleansing shown in Bosnia and Kosovo in several classes of the population in the former Yugoslavia is not just a military operation, but terrorism practiced by militia (the legal nature of the terrorist act is explained in details in the next Chapter).

8. PROPAGANDA IS USED TO MAXIMIZE THE EFFECT OF VIOLENCE, mainly for economic and political reasons. It would be a waste for the terrorist cause if the terrorist operation has no publication. In this meaning, the Black September, during the Olympic Games in Munich in 1972, and all the groups that mirrored that hostage taking, claiming them responsible for attacks in similar circumstances, wanted worldwide publicity for political and economic purposes. From the political point of view, the terrorist group wants to show they are a long-lasting organization, a power to be respected, and a force to be feared. In economic grounds, the group shows to governments that are friendly to its cause and governments that support terrorist groups that it is good enough to receive financial support. Even when terrorists do not publicly take responsibility for the actions, many acts have a particular mode or format that characterizes it, or they leave hints that lead to them.

9. LOYALTY TO THEMSELVES AND TO SYMPATHISERS is a common characteristic of terrorist groups that may be found among

Armenians, Croats, Kurds and Basques, and many others. Within them, loyalty is so intense that they commit unthinkable criminal acts for this loyalty, something that radical elements of a peaceful movement would never do. For the most part, however, the new generations of terrorists have no more a high loyalty on the original cause, the proud to defend it, and a reduced vision of the main objective. Many engage in terrorism to achieve benefits and perpetuation of the criminal activity as the main goal. In conclusion, they become nihilists and interested mainly in the financial return of the activity.

Terrorism during the decades of 1960 and 1970 has been carried on, in its most part, by individuals in college age and political activists with many school years. Today many low intensity conflicts are practiced today by children-soldiers, many of them have not yet in puberty, and become insensible to violence and human emotions.

4.3. PEACEKEEPING AND TERRORISM

Recent peacekeeping has brought an interesting development, bringing a new mission objective to blue helmets: peace operations have gradually incorporated counterterrorism objectives in their mission mandates, and in their operations.

Terrorism is not new, and it has existed during a peacekeeping mission since its beginning. An example is the assassination of Count Folke Bernadotte, UN official for the Arab-Israeli conflict (UNTSO), by the Jewish terrorist group Stern Gang, or Irgun, or Lehi, on September 17th, 1948. Another example happened in the India-Pakistan issue, when groups considered terrorists by one of the sides crossed several times the borders to attack the civilian population, and the Military Observers of UNIPOM had no authority or power to take coercive acts (RAM, Sunil. *The History of United Nations Peacekeeping Operations During the Cold War*, pg. 100).

Separatists in Congo (Katangan Forces, which also fought against ONUC Peacekeepers and the Congolese Central government in 1961, even after the ceasefire). Their terrorist attacks were clearly intended to destabilize the government), according to today's definition of terrorism, have engaged in terrorist acts, deliberately attacking the civilian population for a political purpose. The presence of the UN Mission in the region had the authority to face this threat, even if it is not written in the mandate, because a peacekeeper in the field has the implicit mission to protect the civilian population, within its resources.

However, there is a debate about the definition of terrorism today, despite the similarity of methods, purpose and victims. *Hezbollah* (The Party of God) is considered a terrorist organization by many federal agencies, like the NSA, due to his political objectives and its armed attacks against the Israeli civilian population; but the *Janjaweed* in

Sudan harm in many different ways the civilian population of Darfur, (they are considered one of the responsibles for the genocide in the period 2005-2007) but they are not considered a terrorist group, despite the fact that they have the same motivation of *Hezbollah*, the ethnic cleansing of a region from a population (Jewish people in Lebanon and an ethnic group in Sudan) (JONES, Bruce. *Looking to the Future: Peace Operations in 2015*, pg. 14).

Counterterrorism has already been present in a peace operation in different opportunities. In Afghanistan, ISAF engaged in offensive operations against Taliban, a group considered by the international community as a supporter of terrorism. In the Philippines it was conducted a counterterrorism campaign to stabilize the environment, threatened by the Moro Liberation Front. In Lebanon, UNIFIL's mandate and force capacity has been conceived to engage in counterterrorism operations against *Hezbollah* (SC Res 1701 (2006), drafted after the Israeli-Hezbollah War, Article 1. calls "for a full cessation of hostilities <u>based upon, in particular, the immediate cessation by Hezbollah of all attacks</u>". <www.un.org>).

A peacekeeping mission, robust enough for the mission, may be necessary to prevent spoilers to the peace process, and protect the civilian population against terrorist threats. This is not peace enforcement, another kind of operation that is done when there's no political settlement, and parties to the conflict are to be dealt militarily (no consent in the strategical level). For example, the operations in Afghanistan, the Philippines and Lebanon are peacekeeping, robust enough to fulfill its mandate, because the objective of the operation is in support of a political agreement (JONES, Bruce. *Looking to the Future: Peace Operations in 2015*, pg. 15).

Besides the threat that terrorism poses against the civilian population, there is another reason why a peace operation cannot lack the capacity to face terrorism. The United Nations and its members are a privileged target for a terrorist attack. Kidnapping or murdering a Blue Helmet may cause a lack of political support for the Troop Contributing Country, and bring (or rise) unfriendly propaganda against the Mission in the local and international media.

The United Nations had an impressive setback in Iraq after the attack of the United Nations Headquarters in Baghdad, at August 19th, 2003, when the Special Representative of the Secretary General, the Brazilian Sergio Vieira de Mello, was killed by a vehicle rigged with explosives. The impartiality and credibility of the UN cannot protect the Blue Helmets when the terrorist uses impartial and credible targets to achieve as much media attention and public repulse as possible.

In conclusion, an adequate counterterrorism capability is essential in a peacekeeping mission for two reasons: the Blue Helmets may be targets or victims of terrorism, and also because terror may be used by any party trying to ruin the peace process.

In order to have CT included, a PKO with counterterrorism capability must have (The UN, SC and SG positions about Counter Terrorism and Peace Operations are exposed in Chapter 8):

- Specialized officers in hostage-negotiation, bomb-detection and disarming, security of installations and infrastructures, an assault group and counter-intelligence measures;

- Adequate equipment for surveillance and gathering of intelligence from potential terrorists in the Area of Responsibility of the Mission, and specialized personnel;

- Preview in their mandates of the possibility of deploying these specialized officers and equipment, to work in coordination with the local government;

- Preview in their mandates the use of this intelligence gathered for a criminal prosecution against the persons accused of terrorism.

5. WHAT KIND OF CRIME IS TERRORISM?

From the brief exposition about the concept of terrorism in the previous chapter, we can define in legal terms what kind of crime is this illegal conduct, and the competent courts to prosecute terrorists. A clear and certain mechanism of crime repression is essential to prevent an illegal act, and from this point of view terror is no different than other crimes.

In brief, terrorism is the illegal use, or the illegal threat of using, force or violence against persons or assets, with the intention to coerce or intimidate governments or groups in order to achieve political, religious or ideological objectives.

Terrorism is forbidden by International Humanitarian Law, and it may never be used as a method of warfare. Article 51, § 2, of Additional Protocol I to the Geneva Conventions disposes that, in any circumstances, it is prohibited to commit or threaten to commit violence whose main objective is to disseminate terror among the civilian population.

Although the Law of Armed Conflicts does not specify its definition, a terrorist act, which is strictly forbidden, is different than actions done by regular Armed Forces or guerilla groups that work based on, and in the name of, a hierarchical organization, hold weapons ostensibly during engagement and distinguish themselves from the civilian population.

In Brazil, as in many countries around the world, terror is previewed in the Federal Constitution of 1988, its practice is repudiated (Article 4th, VIII), and is considered unbailable and no amnesty or grace is allowed (Article 5th, XLIII). However, in many countries there is no legal definition of terrorism as a crime, nor the description of a criminal conduct and a punishment for the crime understood as Terrorism. This absence is explained by two reasons.

The first reason is that an act of terrorism is also prescribed in other criminal definitions, like homicide, kidnapping and explosion. But the *animus* (*dolus*, or criminal intention) of the terrorist agent is very different than the common criminal, when he offends the physical integrity, the freedom and the security of the individual. The end of the terrorist is another, and this leads to the second reason.

The intention of the terrorist is to offend the Nation or State, its political or territorial integrity as a Sovereign Nation. Thus, terrorism is committed against a legal entity of public international law, and the conduct must be considered a crime in International Law, because it harms legal rights protected by this branch of law.

The main problem that Rousseau's Social Contract was made to solve is to "find a form of association which will defend and protect with the whole common force the persons and goods of each associate, and in which each, while uniting himself with all, may still obey himself alone, and remain as free as before" (ROUSSEAU, Jean Jacques. *Du Contrat Social*. Université de Nice, 2010).

Terror takes away from the citizen the defense and protection guaranteed by the Social Contract. So, as well as crimes against humanity, war crimes, genocide, aggression, pirating and slavery, terrorism shall be punished by a judge or a Court using the Universal Competence, instead of territorial, material or other criteria of jurisdictional competence, because it is a crime against the Sovereignty of a Nation, and must be punished throughout the world, even if committed in countries that do not have specific laws against it, or in places where there is no Sovereign State to create national laws, like high seas and international airspace (further explanations about jurisdictional competence is provided in Chapter 6).

The examples below corroborate that terrorism is a crime of international law.

An Intra-State warfare in which a guerilla, a rebel faction or any kind of organized group, disguises within the population and does not claim the territory or part of the territory of the Nation, is a Non-International, Asymmetrical and Low Intensity Armed Conflict, when it reaches a level of operability that is higher than mere insurgency. This explanation corresponds to the brief definition of terrorism previously shown.

A "war on terror" is more rhetorical than practical, like "war on hunger", "war on drugs" or "war on crime", because, in order to have a war, there must be at least two belligerents or warring parties. Besides, declaring war is no longer a lawful instrument for international relations (Article 2, § 4, of the UN Charter).

However, a Government may use the right of self-defense, preemptive or real, disposed in Article 51 of the UN Charter, against threats to its territorial integrity or Sovereignty, when they are committed by rebel factions (*Hezbollah* in Lebanon, *Hamas* towards Israel*)*, guerrillas (*Sendero Luminoso* in Peru), and criminal organizations or groups (*Fuerzas Armadas Revolucionarias de Colombia* and *al Qa'ida*).

These entities committed crimes against the integrity of legal entities in international public law (States) or their population (an essential element for a Nation), so they may be prosecuted by international criminal courts. In conclusion, their terrorist acts against States or Nations are considered crimes in international law.

The Rome Statute (that created the International Criminal Court, signed in July 17th, 1998) defines Crimes against Humanity (Article 7 of the Rome Statute) any of the acts below, when executed by an attack, widespread or systematic, against any civilian population, with the specific intention (*dolus specialis*) to commit them (some definitions are not directly related to terrorism, and were omitted):

(a) Murder;

(b) Extermination;

(d) Deportation or forcible transfer of population;

(h) Persecution against any identifiable group;

(i) Enforced disappearance of persons;

(k) Other inhumane acts of a similar character intentionally causing great suffering, or serious injury to body or to mental or physical health.

Crimes against humanity, as defined in the Rome Statute, are a broad legal definition that encompasses many crimes in international law, except those not specifically listed or mentioned. Genocide, for example, would be considered a crime against humanity, but it has a specific criminal definition, in order to distinguish it from the broad term "Crimes against Humanity".

In the same way, widespread and systematic acts of terrorism are crimes included in the broad definition of "Crimes against humanity", according to the definition provided above. Notwithstanding, Terrorism could be prevented and repressed more sharply if the criminal act of "Terrorism" were defined as a crime in international law.

Definitions of terrorism are found in local and international laws (see Chapter 4), but all Members-States had to define terrorism as crimes in their national laws in order to fulfill its terms. However, if we consider terrorism as a crime in international law, only one definition is required, based in international grounds, and it would be applicable to the entire international community.

Even with no specific definition in the Statute of Rome, any of the acts described in Article 7 of the Rome Statute may be considered terrorism (The Draft Code of Crimes against Peace and Security of Mankind, Art. 20, *f,* (iv), refers to acts of terrorism committed in violation of IHL in NIAC as international crimes. According to Brownlie, the draft articles became redundant after the Statute of the International Criminal Court. BROWNLIE, Ian. *Principles*, pg. 561), especially the great suffering or serious injury to body or mental health prescribed in item (k), when committed by an organized group, guerilla or rebel faction.

Guerillas are not terrorist organizations, but when they use terror as a means of warfare against a State or Nation, they are also committing a crime of international law.

Guerillas are combat operations carried on in the territory occupied by the enemy, mainly by military or paramilitary forces of the occupied country.

Guerilleros are allowed to combat (they are legal combatants), and they receive the status of Prisoner of War when captured. They are resistance fighters, militia and volunteer corps that are not part of regular Armed Forces of a country, they operate within or without its own territory, even if this territory is occupied, but they must fulfill four requirements:

- Have a commander responsible for their subordinates (chain of command);

- Have a distinctive sign recognizable at a distance (uniforms, fatigues);

- Hold weapons ostensibly;

- Respect, in their operations, the laws and uses of war.

(Article 4th of the Third Geneva Convention about the treatment of Prisoners of War).

When the guerillero uses illegal methods or means of warfare, terrorism included, he becomes a war criminal, loses the status of Combatant and, when captured, is not considered a Prisoner of War, and shall be prosecuted by an international court, or a national court using the Universal Competence.

On the other hand, the terrorist does not fulfill all the requirements above. He cannot be considered a Prisoner of War, but that doesn't mean he is not a Combatant, due to the obvious fact that there still is an Armed Conflict. So he is an illegal Combatant, using illicit means and methods of warfare.

Any Combatant, recognized as one by International Humanitarian Law, may be considered a Prisoner of War or not, depending on his conduct in the field when he takes up weapons against a Government, a State or a Nation. The terrorist is no different than any combatant in the beginning of the warfare, but at the moment that the agent attacks civilians with the purpose to win the combat through fear among the population, he is no more combating legally, and loses the protection in International Humanitarian Law.

In conclusion, the terrorist is a war criminal, and need to be prosecuted as such (By considering terrorism as a crime in International Law it is created an obligation *erga omnes* to all States to prevent and repress terrorist activities, and prosecute their authors. One State may not claim that terrorism is a not a crime in their national laws, or give asylum/immunity to terrorists).

Another example is the terrorist that uses a civilian as hostage with the *dolus specialis* to bargain with the Government, and also as a human shield during a situation; he is using an illegal method of warfare against a Government for political purposes. This is terrorism when it reaches a great extent and gravity, i.e. a threat to the existence of a State.

In all those cases, may it be judged by a national court? This question may be put in other way: Is the national judge capable and impartial enough to deal with such a crime, when his Motherland, the Population that includes him and his family and friends, the State for which he works, has been harassed?

An economically powerful and democratically strong Nation may not feel a threat to its existence by an explosion of a building, or a kidnapping of a high official of the Government. But feeble States, like those that require the support of a Peace Operation, are much easier to be demolished, and its population is more vulnerable to terrorism.

The roles of national courts that may analyze, prosecute the terrorist act, and punish its authors, and international courts that may perform these tasks, are exposed in the next chapter.

6. ROLE OF LOCAL AND INTERNATIONAL COURTS OF JUSTICE

Once defined that terrorism can be considered a crime in international law for proper judicial repression, five different options are available for the jurisdictional system to prosecute the crime of terrorism:

- begin the legal procedure in a national court, composed of national judges only;

- set up a special criminal court to analyze this specific crime;

- institute an international criminal court, for the same purpose;

- send the case to the International Criminal Court, in The Hague;

- create an hybrid court, with national and international judges, for the case;

From all that has been exposed in the previous chapters, we conclude that the national court (a criminal court of the affected State or Nation) may not prosecute and judge the terrorist properly, for a number of reasons: the public clamor to give the terrorist a severe punishment may spoil the impartiality of the national judge (His impartiality would be granted if the act did not involve him or any of his family or close friends, for example. But this is very unlikely, because a terrorist attack aims the civilian population as a whole). The judge himself may lose his impartiality for the hatred that the terrorist act may cause on him, since he attacked or tried to collapse the political institutions of his motherland.

On the same way, special criminal courts (or special military courts) usually do not have enough independence and impartiality, which may lead to violations of the right to a fair trial, and/or limited access to lawyers, witnesses and other means to prove his innocence.

Example: Special Court for Sierra Lione, created in 2006 to prosecute and judge Charles Taylor, under the accusation of 11 counts of war crimes and crimes against humanity. His presence in Liberia threatened the fragile peace process, and he was transferred to the Hague for prosecution (RAM, Sunil. *The History of UN Peacekeeping Operations From Retrenchment to Resurgence*, pg. 168).

Making justice outside the rule of law is mere revenge, and it does not prevent terrorism. On the contrary, it insufflates the hatred by other persons against the vengeful government, creating a vicious circle of violence between the Government and the armed opposition, in which the population suffers the centrifugal force in the center.

A crime in international law requires a prosecution and judgment by a court using the Universal Competence, which is granted to any federal court (The judicial competence for analyzing severe Human Rights violations is usually given to Federal Courts because, in these cases, the State may have disrespected an obligation in international law (for example, from the ICCPR, GA Res. 16 Dec 1996). Ex: Art. 109, §5º, Brazilian Constitution. Ex: U.S. Bill of Rights) court of a government). However, in order to guarantee the Due Process of Law when prosecuting crimes that have caused a common and widespread feeling of repulse and indignation, we must learn from the previous experiences and lessons from the past.

6.1. INTERNATIONAL CRIMINAL COURTS

The International Criminal Tribunal for the former Yugoslavia (ICTY) was created by Security Council Resolution 827, of May 25 1993, based on Chapter VII of the UN Charter. It had competence to prosecute individuals responsible for high breaches of International Humanitarian Law committed in the territory of ex-Yugoslavia since 1991, according to dispositions of its Statute (Article 1 of the Statute of International Criminal Tribunal for the former Yugoslavia).

The jurisdiction of the ICTY was limited to grave violations of the Geneva Conventions, in other words, violations to the laws and uses of war, crimes of genocide and crimes against humanity committed in the territory of the former Yugoslavia since January 1st, 1991.

Despite its parallel jurisdiction with national tribunal of each State Party, the ICTY had primary jurisdiction and could request that national tribunals renounce their competence. According to the Principle of *non bis in idem* (the person cannot be condemned more than once for the same crime), cases already prosecuted and judged by a national tribunal could not be reanalyzed by ICTY. However, by derogation, so that nobody escapes from its criminal responsibility, the author may be submitted again to the ICTY if the *factum delicti* was described as a crime of national law, if the decision was not impartial or independent, or if the procedure against him was not carried on properly.

The ICTY was able to convict to prison, in the same way as other national courts in the former Yugoslavia, but could not convict to a death sentence. It was also able to determinate the restitution of properties achieved by illegal methods to its lawful owners. The judges were elected by UN General Assembly, after propositions of the States of which they are nationals.

The International Criminal Tribunal for Rwanda (ICTR) was created on November 8th, 1994 by SC Resolution 955 using Chapter VII of the UN Charter, the ICTR was competent to prosecute individuals responsible for acts of genocide, crimes against humanity, violations of Common Article 3 of the Geneva Convention and its Additional Protocol II, or other grave breaches to International Humanitarian Law, committed on the territory of Rwanda and on the territory of neighboring countries, between January 1st to December 31st, in accordance to the dispositions of its Statute (Statute of International Criminal Tribunal for Rwanda, Art. 1).

The ICTR, similarly to ICTY, has the same competence as the national criminal courts, it had prime jurisdiction, and it had power to bring to analysis cases from the competence of national courts. Like ICTY, the Principle of *non bis in idem* did not apply in the same cases (prosecuted as common crime, unfair or non independent trial). It was able to convict to the same crimes as national judges (besides death penalty) and determine restitution of property to its owners.

6.2. THE INTERNATIONAL CRIMINAL COURT

In the sequence to the events that took place in ex-Yugoslavia and Rwanda, the international community realized that it was necessary to increase the international crime repression through international penal instruments, with the creation of two *ad hoc* (for the case) international courts for Ex-Yugoslavia (ICTY) and Rwanda (ICTR) and, recently, created the International Criminal Court (Created by Rome Statute, in July 17th, 1998. The ICC Draft Statute was recommended to the General-Assembly in 1994 by many delegations, because it would be more appropriate than the *ad hoc* regional tribunals created by the Security Council. BROWNLIE, Ian. *Principles*, pg. 571). While the ICTY and ICTR became active right after their creation, the ICC began its activities the first day of the following month after the deposit of the sixtieth ratification of its funding Treaty (Statute of Rome). In other words, it is active since July 1st, 2002.

Article 1 of the Statute of Rome disposes that it is created an International Criminal Court, a permanent institution, which may exert its jurisdiction on individuals, concerning crimes of high concern in international jurisdiction. Its jurisdiction is complementary to the role of national criminal judges.

The jurisdiction of the court is restricted to very serious crimes that affect the international community as a whole. In the terms of its Statute (Article 1, § 5 of Statute of Rome), the Court has jurisdiction on the following crimes:

- Genocide (destroy, in whole or in part, a national, ethnical, racial or religious group, through killing members of the group, or causing serious bodily or mental harm, or inflicting conditions on the life calculated to bring about its physical destruction in whole or in part, or imposing measures to prevent births within the group, or forcibly transferring children of the group to another group);

- Crimes against humanity (widespread or systematic attacks directed against any civilian population, like murder, extermination, enslavement, deportation or forcible transfer of population, imprisonment or other severe deprivation of physical liberty in violation of fundamental rules of international law, torture, rape, sexual slavery, enforced prostitution, forced pregnancy, enforced sterilization, or any other form of sexual violence of comparable gravity, persecution against any identifiable group or collectivity on political, racial, national, ethnic, cultural, religious, gender, or other grounds that are universally recognized as impermissible under international law, in connection with any act considered a crime against humanity or any crime within the jurisdiction of the ICC);

- War crimes (grave breaches of the Geneva Conventions of 12 August 1949, against persons or property protected under the provisions of the relevant Geneva Conventions, like willful killing, torture or inhuman treatment, including biological experiments, willfully causing great suffering, or serious injury to body or health, extensive destruction and appropriation of property, not justified by military necessity and carried out unlawfully and wantonly, compelling a prisoner of war or other protected person to serve in the forces of a hostile power, willfully depriving a prisoner of war or other protected person of the rights of fair and regular trial, unlawful deportation, transfer or confinement, taking of hostages);

- Crime of aggression (plan, prepare, initiate or wage a war of aggression, or a war in violation of international treaties, agreements or assurances, or participation in a common plan or conspiracy for the accomplishment of the foregoing).

The Statute of the Court was approved in Rome, on June 17th, 1998. Different than the International Court of Justice (ICJ), that analyses litigations between States, the International Criminal Court is competent to prosecute individuals accused of particularly severe crimes: genocide, crimes against humanity, war crimes and crimes of aggression. The ICC exerts its jurisdiction only when the State of the nationality of the accused, or the State whose territory the crime has happened, is part of the Convention, or explicitly gives its consent. The Tribunal is supplementary to national courts. The Court shall intervene only when the national tribunals cannot or refuse to bring the responsible persons to trial.

The ICC may begin the prosecution when provoked by States Parties, by UN Security Council or *ex* officio, with previous authorization of the Preliminary Chamber. Different than other International Criminal Tribunals and Courts (limited in time and territory), the ICC may exert its competence and jurisdiction in the territory of any State Party and, through a special agreement, in the territory of any State.

The ICC judges are elected by the UN General Assembly, from a list created by the Security Council, after a proposition by the State of which they are nationals.

Article 89 of the Statute of Rome creates an important institute: the Surrender. The ICC may send a demand of detention and surrender of an individual, instructed with documents referred in Article 91, to any country in whose territory this person may be, and require cooperation from this State in the detention and surrender of this individual. The States-Parties will respond to requests of detention and surrender according to Chapter Nine (International Cooperation and Judicial Assistance) and proceed according to the national rules.

This juridical instrument has been created to avoid the problems of Extradition, and only the ICC may use the request of Surrender, in crimes of its competence. The State party may refuse the request of Surrender only when the accused is already been prosecuted for the same crime, or it has already been judged (condemning or absolving) about the same case.

6.3. INTERNATIONALIZED CRIMINAL JURISDICTION

Third Generation of International Criminal Jurisdiction, the Internationalized Criminal Tribunals, or Hybrid Criminal Tribunals, are another option for the prosecution of crimes in International Law. It is also called International Criminal Justice of Proximity.

This branch of Criminal Justice addresses the jurisdictional mechanisms that national judges work side by side with international judges, applying the legislation of the country where the illicit facts were committed, allowing the participation of the State and its population in the procedure that will condemn or absolve the accused of international crimes.

The main advantage of this methodology is to be close to the community that has witnessed the crimes committed. Nevertheless, they are *ad hoc* judges, using the Universal Competence, nominated to assure the certitude of the procedure, especially in crimes in which there is a high internal pressure that may influence the impartiality of the national judge.

Another great advantage is the fast and easy hearing of witnesses, and production of proofs by both parties, because they are near the judges, and the Court may use the national judiciary system to do arrests, citations and intimations. Besides, a correct, impartial and fair trial seen by the whole population may cause a deterrence effect in other potential terrorists.

The trial by Internationalized Criminal Courts is based on the internal competence of the State, concerning the matter, the person or the place (*ratione materiae, personae* or *loci*), but also based on the Universal Competence. Therefore, there is no offense to the Sovereignty of the State, avoiding the main problem of the application of the Universal Competence alone.

Example: Tribunals in Cambodia, for the prosecutions of Khmers Rouges, with three national judges and two international judges, and Appeal Chamber with four national judges and three international judges.

Example: Tribunal in Lebanon, for the judgment of the assassination of Premier Rafic Hariri, with two international judges and one Lebanese, and Appeal Chamber with three international judges and two Lebanese ones.

6.4. INTERNATIONAL JUSTICE AND PEACEKEEPING

The confluence between the work of International Criminal Judges and the Blue Helmets is evident: they are created by the Security Council, they have clear and specific mandates, derived from Chapter VII of the Charter, a limited duration, and their main goal is to restore and maintain international peace and security, the same objective as the United Nations (Charter, Article 1, §1).

From all branches of International Law, the IHL is considered to be the most theoretical and the most difficult norm to be implemented. At the time when there were no criminal tribunals to prosecute the offenders of IHL, this branch of law was more rhetorical than practical. Today this cannot be accepted anymore, especially concerning crimes that present threats to international peace and security, like terrorism.

It is likely that not all cases of terrorist may be brought to the International Criminal Court in The Hague, because many of them lack the requisite of most serious crimes of international concern. In these cases, a specific International or Internationalized Criminal Court is the solution for a fair, fast and impartial prosecution of terrorists.

Also, when the host country does not, or cannot, provide means for the International Criminal Court or similar Tribunals to fulfill the mandates (mainly arrest and citation of terrorists, but also Preliminary Investigations and Inquiries), the Blue Helmets may perform the task, when duly authorized in their mandates by the Security Council.

With the modern internalization of armed conflicts the International Humanitarian Law has become more difficult to be respected, by national military (claiming that it decreases battle efficiency) and rebel factions (due to the lack of discipline). Also, IHL is considered the branch of Law that has few means of implementation, and only among States (through treaties, conciliation, mediation and other diplomatic efforts).

The Trial of Major War Criminals in Nuremberg has declared, about the implementation of International Criminal Law, that international law imposes duty and liabilities upon individuals as well as upon States, and both could be punished for violations of international law. Crimes, international or not, are committed by men, not by abstract entities, and only by punishing individuals who commit such crimes can the provisions of international law be enforced.

All international entities must respect State Sovereignty. However, when this State does not meet its obligations to protect internationally recognized human rights (Libya, during the government of Muammar Kaddafi, and Syria, during the government of Bashar al-Assad, are two notorious cases of HR violations, which demanded a response from the international community), the Security Council or other competent entity may prosecute individuals from that State, disregarding the Sovereignty, in application of the principle *Hominum causa omne jus constitutum est* (All law is created for the benefit of human beings).

It is difficult to assemble a branch of consensual and theoretical law (International Humanitarian Law) with practical and coercive legal procedures (that are within the Criminal Law). In this context lies the main role of International Criminal Tribunals, punishing the violations of IHL, using doctrinal and abstract definitions to make concrete and coercive decisions, and in this way dissuading terrorism from happening again.

To be efficient, the decisions of International Criminal Courts must have:

- Dissuasion, because only a rigorous application of International Humanitarian Law can make warring parties respect it;

- Individual responsibility, in order to avoid collective guilt and ostracism by one ethnic or national group and the desire of vengeance, making conditions for national reconciliation;

- Search for the truth, so that history be written as much exact as possible, protecting the concerned people over revisionism, creating conditions for a durable peace.

Blue Helmets may work as an executive arm of International Criminal Tribunals, bringing terrorists to prosecution and trial, and also doing investigations, arrests, citations, intimations and other mandates drafted by the International Criminal Court, or other international criminal organs, when the mandate has expressly given them the power to prevent and repress crimes of international law, and the duty to work as the *longa manus* of International Criminal Courts or Tribunals.

Example: Due to the immunity given by Nigeria to Charles Taylor, and the repeated refusal to turn in to the Special Court in Sierra Lione, United Nations Mission in Liberia (UNIMIL)'s mandate was changed by SC Res. 1638 (2005), to "apprehend and detain former president Charles Taylor in the event of a return to Liberia and to transfer him or facilitate his transfer to Sierra Lione for prosecution before the Special Court for Sierra Lione and to keep the Liberian government, the Sierra Lionean Government and the Council fully informed". He was arrested in March, 26th, 2006 (RAM, Sunil. *The History of UN Peacekeeping Operations From Retrenchment to Resurgence*, pg. 169).

Example: Jean-Pierre Bemba Gombo, former senator in the Democratic Republic of Congo, was arrested near Brussels by Belgian authorities, following an arrest warrant drafted by the International Criminal Court. He was arrested on May, 24th, 2008 (BBC News, 24 May 2008, <news.bbc.co.uk>).

The examples given show that the main obstacle to prosecute violators of International Humanitarian Law is the absence of cooperation between the competent International Criminal Courts and some governments that do not follow arrest warrants for criminals in their jurisdiction. When there is no cooperation for arresting criminals, a Peace Operation would perform the task, since it has a civilian component capable to address the issue, and a military component to provide necessary means of security.

The exigency of justice is essential to make the absence of conflicts (negative peace) become a reconciled society (positive peace). Peacekeepers and ICC may work together for it.

7. THE UN CHARTER, PRINCIPLES AND ORGANS

The United Nations was created in 1945, with the signature and ratification of the Charter in San Francisco. The historical background of the creation of the UN System lies in the aftermath of World War II and the efforts of the League of Nations to make a peaceful mechanism to settle disputes among States.

The UN Charter disposes all duties and rights of Member States, its major principles and organs. Article 1 sets the main goals of the Organization, in order to prevent future generations from the scourge of war:

- Maintain international peace and security;
- Develop friendly relations among States;
- Achieve international cooperation in order to solve disputes of economic, social, intellectual or humanitarian issues;
- Develop and improve the respect of human rights and fundamental freedoms, with no distinction of race, gender, language or religion;
- Harmonize the efforts of Nations towards common ends.

In order to achieve its goals, the UN shall follow the principles announced in Article 2:

- Equal sovereignty of all its Members;
- Good faith to accomplish its obligations;
- Peaceful methods to settle disputes;
- Abstention to use force or the threat of force in international relations (i. e., war is no longer a valid continuation of international politics for other ways);
- Give support to any UN action according to the Charter;
- Abstention from assisting a State against which the UN has taken preventive or coercive measures;

- Non-Members States are demanded to take any needed measures for the maintenance of international peace and security;

- Non-intervention in affairs concerning the internal competence of States, except the coercive measures of Chapter VII.

The Charter bases the UN action in four main areas: peace and security, economic and social issues, the trusteeship system, and the judicial organ. Six organs were created to accomplish its goals: the General Assembly, the Security Council, the Social and Economic Council, the Trusteeship Council, the International Court of Justice and the Secretariat.

The first challenge of the UN System was to deal with the struggle between the two superpowers (characterized by their influence in international relations and the possession of great warfare capability, including nuclear weapons), the United States of America (USA) and the Union of Soviet Socialist Republics (USSR).

This struggle was the Cold War, which lasted until 1991. During that time, threats to international peace and security could not have a response from the organ mainly concerned, the Security Council. The two superpowers used the power of veto to prevent the SC from analyzing and adopting measures of collective security (employment of armed forces and other coercive tools).

When conciliatory methods for the settlement of disputes do not work, or are not available (Chapter VI) and the collective security system of coercive action in cases of menace or breaches to peace are not available (Chapter VII), the solution was to create the alternative of peacekeeping, based in a "Chapter VI and a half" that uses both legal norms and powers.

The History of UN Peace Operations, from its beginning in 1948 to the present days, has already been exposed. Now it is time for a fourth step towards international peace and security, by including in multidimensional peacekeeping mission a counterterrorism capability, and also add responsibilities to other UN organs and agencies concerned.

7.1. THE GENERAL ASSEMBLY (GA)

The GA is the main deliberative organ, comprised of all UN Members. It can make recommendations to Member States or the Security Council on any questions related to the objectives of the Charter, exemption made when the CS is already examining the case, or has already taken a decision.

Thus, threats or breaches to international peace and security may be analyzed by the GA, when the SC is not informed of it yet. It may also take a decision in important issues by the favorable votes of two thirds of its Members.

A recommendation concerning counterterrorism may be discussed in GA First Committee (Disarmament and International Security) and Sixth Committee (Legal Affairs).

7.2. THE SECURITY COUNCIL (SC)

It is the prime responsible for the maintenance of international peace and security. It may take action using the powers of Chapter VI (negotiation, investigation, mediation, conciliation, arbitration, judicial settlement, resort to regional agreements and organisms, or other peaceful means).

The SC may also take coercive methods previewed in Chapter VII, that is, to demand Member States to do the following:

- Complete or partial interruption of economic relations;

- Interruption of railway, aerial, postal, telegraphic, radioelectric communications;

- Rupture of diplomatic relations;

- Embargoes (prohibition to sell weapons, petrol, vehicles and other items).

If the coercive methods above have not taken effect, or are inadequate, it may take or authorize aerial, naval or terrestrial operations to do:

- Demonstrations of strength (mobilizing troops and vehicles in the border, making airstrikes, seizing or sinking warships);

- Blockades in routes, ports and airports, except humanitarian help for the population;

- Authorize a Peace Operation, using military and police troops from Member States (Troop Contributing Countries).

In order to have a counterterrorism capacity in Peace Operations, the SC must provide a mandate with specific powers to peacekeepers: Rules of Engagement (ROE) enabling them to act in cases of terrorism and other international crimes; authorization to comply with mandates from International Criminal Courts; and require that Troop Contributing Countries send some of their military with special training concerning counterterrorism.

7.3. THE ECONOMIC AND SOCIAL COUNCIL (ECOSOC)

The ECOSOC has the role to make recommendations concerning economic, social, cultural, health development, assurance and improvement. They may be addressed to the GA, Member States or specialized agencies.

Among its many Commissions, Crime Prevention and Criminal Justice, Human Rights, Narcotics and Drugs are related to terrorism matters, and may conduct studies about measures to detect and prevent it.

7.4. THE TRUSTEESHIP COUNCIL (TC)

The TC was responsible for the administration and supervision of territories in order to promote development and progress towards independence. Trusted territories were territories under mandates during the League of Nations, or detached from enemy states after WW II, or placed voluntarily.

Today there are no more territories under its supervision, but the General Assembly recommended that the TC analyses cases concerning the integrity of the global environment, the ocean, atmosphere and outer space, and also modification in the environment (UNITED NATIONS, <www.un.org/documents/tc.htm>).

7.5. THE INTERNATIONAL COURT OF JUSTICE (ICJ)

The ICJ is the main judicial organ of the UN. Its main roles are to settle disputes submitted to it by Member States, according to international law, and give advisory opinions to the General Assembly, the Security Council and, when authorized by the General Assembly, to other UN organs and agencies.

Concerning terrorism, it may give a number of advisory opinions and judgments, from the legality of establishing an International or Internationalized Criminal Court, or sending the case to the International Criminal Court, or even whether or not the terrorist act in study may be considered a breach or rupture or international peace and security.

7.6. THE SECRETARIAT AND THE SECRETARY GENERAL (SG)

The administrative work of the United Nation is carried on by the Secretariat, which is headed by the Secretary General. It is divided in offices, departments and Special Representatives. Its staff implements programs and policies decided by the other five organs.

It is the closest organ to a peacekeeping mission, and its roles concerning it vary from the talks to Troop Contributing Countries in order to send military personnel to a Peace Operation, to information sent to the Security Council about the situation in the field that Blue Helmets are experiencing, with recommendations to change the mandate or to extend the mission.

The Secretary-General has the responsibility to inform to the Security Council of any potential threat to international peace and security, and also other functions entrusted to him by any UN organs. Since he is usually chosen in the diplomatic community, he is also entrusted to bring warring parties to the dialogue through good offices.

In brief, there is no need for a structural change to perform tasks specifically related to terrorism, because all UN System was conceived to deal with international peace and security, and it is a very flexible system, that has adapted itself to face new challenges throughout its history. All the UN need is another review of its doctrine, in order to face the challenges of the 21st Century.

8. UN EFFORTS AGAINST TERRORISM

Three weeks after the terrorist attacks on the World Trade Center, the Pentagon and the hijacking of another plane that crashed on land, on September 11, 2001, the U.N. Security Council approved Resolution 1373. It is an uncommon document because for the first time a resolution based on Chapter VII was created to apply to all U.N. Member States. It aims criminal, financial, and administrative measures to bring to an end the support of individuals and entities involved in terrorism.

Resolution 1373 (2001), of September 28, 2001, request that states avoid and restrain the financial support of terrorist acts through very austere legal and financial procedures; to cease providing any form of sustainment to parties related to terrorism; to set up terrorist acts as grave criminal conducts in national legislation, with severe punishment; and to establish procedures to check for potential terrorists before granting refugee status to them, when they are involved in planning, participation or commission of terrorist acts.

The Counter Terrorism Committee (CTC) was put in place with Resolution 1373 (2001) to supervise the implementation of these measures, as well as to enhance the ability of governments to combat terrorism. All members of the Security Council are part to the CTC. Resolution 1373 demands that all States inform the CTC about the adoption of the measures, showing what procedures they had created to comply with the resolution, all with a deadline of 90 days.

There is no reference in Resolution 1373 about the respect of international human rights, humanitarian and refugee law. This situation was ended by Security Council Resolution 1456 of January 20, 2003, requiring states to guarantee that procedures in the struggle against terrorism are done in accordance with all related dispositions in international law. It also required the adoption of measures to comply with international law, especially international human rights, refugee and humanitarian law. Resolution 1456 is an important binding and a step forward to uphold respect with international human rights values.

The Counterterrorism Executive Directorate (CTED) was created in March 2004 to grant institutional help to the counterterrorism engagement. The CTED has a staff of experts to give advisory opinions to the CTC about technical aspects of government's reports.

Reports to CTC shall firstly relate progress in the placement of legislation to apply all measures of Resolution 1373, and steps taken to become a party to international conventions and protocols concerning terrorism; also, inform about the implementation of effective administrative measures for preventing and repressing the financing of terrorism.

A later stage in the reports shall bring executive structures (police, intelligence, and also customs, immigration and border controls; allowing no access to military hardware) in order to prevent new recruits to terrorist groups, their gathering, safe places or other supportive measures for terrorist members or groups.

The working methodology of the CTC and CTED comprise:

- Visits to countries to evaluate the nature and assistance given to comply with SC Res 1737, and monitor their progress;

- Programs of technical, financial, regulatory and legislative assistance, to link countries;

- Complete Reports for countries concerning counterterrorism circumstances, and also become a dialogue channel to the Committee;

- Best practices, codes and standards so governments may apply them according to their necessities and obligations;

- Meeting with international and regional organizations, in order to reach unity of effort and use resources the best way as possible.

Terrorism is a real threat in a number of countries around the world. However, its counter methods must observe the core values of the international legal system. All instruments and directives available to countries shall be used to prevent the dissemination of terror.

In short, combating terrorism must not cause terror to the population concerned or the terror will continue with other actors. So, in order to avoid that, international law needs to be obeyed, and humanitarian law must be observed with no exceptions.

Some countries argue that it is necessary to implement special powers to respond to the unprecedented and exceptional threat of terrorism. Those special powers may include:

- Broad and subjective definitions of terrorism that are similar to political crimes;

- Power to arrest and detain persons without a judicial warrant;

- Enter houses without a judicial warrant or a state of flagrancy;

- Break the secrecy of communication and correspondence without a judicial warrant;

- Maintain detained persons *incommunicado* even for their parents and lawyer;

- Maintain temporary detention for indefinite time;

- Bring terrorist to *ad hoc* or military courts;

- Use methods of inquiring that may seem like torture;

- Use intelligence obtained illegally in an investigation.

At the strategic level, the worldwide effort against terrorism is well-planed by the Security Council and other international actors concerned, well-oriented and effective. Today it is very difficult for a country or organization to give support to terrorists, finance illegal groups, and organize training camps for recruits, because State-Parties and/or the international community will penalize him with embargoes, restraints in economic and diplomatic affairs.

At the tactical level, however, the special powers given to prevent terror, usually not followed by accountability on administrative and criminal grounds for the misconduct of government agents, have caused a great fear in the population. Causing fear in a population, especially when this originates ostracism and detachment of minorities, is counterproductive and against all efforts to combat terrorism. It is not effective to combat fear with more fear.

9. THE ROLE OF INTELLIGENCE IN COUNTERTERRORISM

Intelligence can be defined as the operation of gathering information of an enemy, in the context of an Armed Conflict. Gathering intelligence is indispensable in preventing terrorism, since it can identify, understand and analyze terrorist menaces before they happen, and create material basis for criminal investigations and prosecutions, and also to build up preventive strategies. This is an essential function in a democratic country, since it enables fair trials, and is known for centuries.

However, now the powers and available procedures of intelligence agencies, with international share of information and an unprecedented cooperation to track terrorists and follow their activities, have led to a multiplicity of legal and administrative procedures that prioritize collective security in detriment to individual liberties.

It is a State responsibility to protect their citizens from any collective attack, and it is notorious that intelligence gathering is the only available instrument to prevent threats to the population. Also, terrorist actors that have supporters in other countries can be much better fought when all concerned governments, and their agencies, work together.

It is also doubtless that intelligence gathering must be confidential, not open to public scrutiny, in order to protect their operations, intelligence agents and, more important, the individuals investigated. New electronic devices and international cooperation have brought intelligence to the core of any counterterrorism effort, but this cannot bring lack of accountability for those who exceed in the use of investigative powers.

The separation of powers, characterized by the system of checks and balances among the Executive, Legislative and Judiciary, more than ever needs to be respected. Intelligence cannot make the Executive powers heavier and more important than the others.

In the same way, the rule of law (*État de droit*) and the due process of law, comprising respectively individual freedoms (communication, association, opinion, and others), and judicial guarantees (contradict the accusation, presumption of innocence, production of proofs, non acceptance of proofs illegally produced) are necessary to protect innocent people from misinterpreted intelligence and unfair trials.

Accountability is necessary to counterbalance the powers given to intelligence actors that abuse from their executive authority. Surely, if the activity requires secrecy, so does the legal procedure. The confidentiality of the prosecution is needed to protect the agents, their families and also the victim of illegal or abusive investigation. Compensation for the victim is also necessary, but the fact that the person understands the consequences of abusing from their powers, and the certainty that he will be punished, prevents him from misconduct.

The gathering of intelligence is always a potential threat to individual intimacy. Intelligence operations need to be secret, and so their sources. However, the transparency of the rule of law may be granted, not disclosing operational methods, but who the decision-maker of the abuse is, how the decision was taken, and what measures were taken to prevent, or punish, corruption, misuse of information or illegality.

The increase of executive powers by the Executive is also a potential ground for misconduct. All intelligence agencies have a daily report to their superiors, but there is no supervision from judicial organs. Also, close surveillance and law enforcement measures, like arrest, detention and interrogation, requires a judicial warrant to be in the due process of law.

When agents privilege intelligence, they are likely to take an opportunity to arrest a suspect, intercept his communications (mail, email, or phone) or invade his domicile outside the rule of law (no flagrant of crime or judicial warrant). This will happen only if there is no accountability, or no expectation of punishment.

The international cooperation among international agencies brought a new danger to the rule of law and judicial system: the share of proofs without knowing how it has been produced. Since the exchange of information is encouraged, an investigation may be carried on with proofs gathered in other countries.

Example: the legal system of the country A permits a mail interception without a judicial warrant. So the proof was legal in national law, although it may lead to an unfair trial. This proof may be used to require an extradition to country B, which forbids this illegal procedure. If the extradition is granted, the B country will have used illegal proofs, disfiguring the due process of law granted in country B.

In some cases the extradition is granted even when the person may be subject to mistreatments due to his race, religion, nationality, political opinion or for participating in a certain group. This condition prevents him from being extradited, according to the Principle of Non-Refoulement.

In some procedures, when there is not enough proof for a prosecution, the extradition has been replaced to rendition. The rendition is required for intelligence gathering, and the suspect is sent to the foreign country for interrogation, with no advice to his family. However, without a legal procedure, the rendition is forced disappearance, a crime in international law.

The Terrorist Surveillance Program (TSP), conducted by the National Security Agency (NSA) in the United States, operating sometime after Sep 11th but known only since 2005, permitted electronic close watch of potential members of Al Qaida, or connected groups, without a judicial warrant when one of the persons involved was outside the US. The TSP was in conflict with the previous Foreign Intelligence Surveillance Act, and the new regulation was confirmed later. All tracking of communications outside the US does not require judicial authorization and scrutiny, even if one person in the US is involved (REPORT OF THE INTERNATIONAL COMMISSION OF JURISTS, 2008, pg. 83).

The powers of investigation and arrest without a judicial warrant shall be exceptional, temporary and require enough suspicion based on previous information and data gathered. In no way they may be used in everyday investigation, even when the integrity of a Nation is concerned. The international cooperation against terrorism includes, besides intelligence sharing, law enforcement and immigration measures.

Among the issues that the gathering of intelligence arises in what concerns the legality of an interrogation are:

- No identification of the interrogators;

- The absence of a lawyer during the suspect's interrogation;

- The right to intervene, through a lawyer, in unclear or ambiguous questions;

- The right to inform the family of his detention;

- The right to not respond to any questions he does not want to answer;

- The right to deny answering a question with no presumption against him;

- The right to choose a lawyer of his own choice (he is appointed by the interrogator);

- The communication in confidence with the counselor;

- Detention with no time limits, or repeatedly renewed;

- Detention by executive powers, with no judicial confirmation;

- No access to legal remedies, like *Habeas Corpus*, to discuss the detention in a court;

- Impossibility to require agents to testimony in court.

Violations may take place not only when the intelligence is gathered, but mainly when there are no specific criteria or regulations about the access and use of such information. A database information system with no clear specifications and description may refer to a national as a terrorist threat, and share this information. When the national travels abroad, or makes business overseas, he will be misjudged as a potential threat and suffer from delays in immigrations, bank transfers and even mail delivery.

The legal aspects in the conduction of an investigation about terrorist activities and the treatments of detainees will be discussed in the next Chapter.

Personal knowledge about a person is usually a sensitive issue, and they may be used for purposes other than criminal investigation, or sent to third countries or to agents with no national accountability in their national judicial system.

The first legal rule in intelligence services, concerning secrecy and confidentiality is that, when a person discloses any sensitive information, it becomes responsible to maintain this intelligence secret or confidential from the public or the media. In other words, he/she is accountable in their judicial system in administrative and criminal grounds.

In conclusion, proper accountability is the only way to prevent abuses in intelligence gathering services, and it is a responsibility of both sender and receiver countries of the information, independent of his national legal framework.

10. IHL: THE PROBLEM OR THE SOLUTION?

With the power of detention (previously explained) comes the right to interrogate the suspect, which is also part of any investigation. However, in some cases persons suspected with terrorist activities are held outside the rule of law, in secret or *incommunicado* detention and without access to a lawyer, their families or judicial remedies like *habeas corpus*, among other concerns already exposed.

It is also said about different methods of interrogations that may be interpreted as torture, among others that are clearly illegal in international human rights law.

They are both performed with the purpose of gathering intelligence in sensitive situations, when any connection between the detained and the outside may spoil the investigation and bring a threat to the country, when the suspect really is a terrorist and may order a bomb attack or an assassination.

All this discussion takes place because of the use of the Human Rights legal framework, which is not the most adequate tool when a Government deals with enemies in a Non-International, Asymmetrical, Low Intensity Armed Conflict, where the parties are the Government and the terrorist group.

In this situation the correct legal framework is the International Humanitarian Law. Thus, any member of one party (Government or terrorist group) may be considered a Combatant, and be granted the status of Prisoner of War until there is enough ground to affirm he has committed a crime in international law (terrorism or other crimes against humanity). Therefore a legal process can begin in a court competent to deal with such offenses.

Only then his condition will change from Prisoner of War to War Criminal, because there is enough proof he has committed a crime (using illegal methods of combat, causing widespread terror to the population), and the prosecution against him may begin.

When there is doubt about the detainee's status, he shall be considered a Prisoner of War, because any person engaged in combat must have it granted, until proper clarification.

When there is sufficient evidence that terror was used, or is planned to be used, against the civilian population, and it is clear that terrorism is an illegal method of warfare, there is enough data to affirm that there is an Armed Conflict, and the detained involved in terrorism is a potential Combatant, and a potential Prisoner of War if detained.

A Prisoner of War is defined as any Combatant that falls in the hand of the enemy, be it in a regular Armed Force, a guerrilla, an insurrectional group or a terrorist. In order to be a Combatant, the person must have the requisites below (already explained in Chapter Five):

- Have a commander responsible for their subordinates (chain of command);

- Have a distinctive sign recognizable at a distance (uniforms, fatigues);

- Holding weapons ostensibly;

- Respecting, in their operations, the laws and uses of war.

While a potential terrorist is considered a combatant, surveillance procedures, interception of communication and individual arrest and detention for interrogation, all with no judicial mandate, are executive legal methods to gather intelligence of the enemy, and within the legal scope of International Humanitarian Law and the Law of Armed Conflict.

When a person suspected of terrorism is detained, the status of Prisoner of War must be granted to him, because he is a legal Combatant until there is enough evidence that he committed crimes in regard of international law.

As a Prisoner of War, he will receive the proper treatment, in the following terms:

- He will be detained until the end of hostilities against that group, because he cannot be released and join the Adverse Party again;

- He has no access to judicial writs like *Habeas Corpus*, or to lawyers, but he is not considered as having committed any crime in national law;

- He cannot communicate with any other person than the representative of the Red Cross and Red Crescent Movement, in order not to give sensitive information to the Adverse Party (the terrorist group or affiliated persons);

- He will be treated humanely, and in no way be obliged to answer any questions during his interrogation; and

- He will in no hypothesis be tortured, and confessions given by torture will be declared null and void, with overall compensation for the individual.

However, when there is enough basis for the accusation of participation or action in a terrorist act, his status will change from Prisoner of War to a Criminal (for terrorism or crimes against humanity) in International Law, because s/he did not fulfill the requirements to be a POW: he did not respect the law and rules of war when he used illegal methods of warfare by causing widespread terror in the civilian population.

Also, s/he did not distinguish him/herself from the civilian population, because s/he did not wear uniforms or fatigues, which is a violation of the Principle of Discrimination; neither did s/he hold his weapons ostensibly. Those are clear examples of Perfidy, a violation of IHL.

Then, the alleged criminal will be prosecuted by an international (or internationalized) Court for the crimes committed. If there is not enough evidence for prosecution, s/he will be released.

However, in any cases he must be treated humanely, i.e., not tortured nor suffering from cruel, inhuman or degrading treatment. If he is considered a national criminal, he will be sent to national court to prosecution. In no way inhumane handling is acceptable.

The case concerning the death of Osama bin Laden is a clear example of how the correct legal framework can influence the legitimacy of an operation. He used one of his wives as a human shield to resist the arrest (According to the unofficial version of the scene. ABC News May 02, 2011, <www.abcnews.go.com>). In the end the Military Objective has been achieved, but there was a collateral damage, the death of the human shield.

If one tries to analyze the case from the human rights framework, the operation was completely illegal, because in HR law there is no collateral damage. Negotiation or other non-lethal methods should have been used, and siege all the compound until he gives up, or there is an opportunity to neutralize him with no risk to the hostage, or the hostage is in clear and immediate danger. But this is not a feasible point of view.

However, if the observer studies the case using the International Humanitarian Law framework, bin Laden was considered a Combatant, so a Military Objective, and his neutralization was considered a Military Necessity. There was no time for a siege, or negotiation, because it was a situation that required a swift decision. The death of the human shield, although unfortunate, was a collateral damage proportional to the Objectives achieved.

Bin Laden could be arrested and go to a trial in an International Court for Crimes in International Law (Although international courts have subsidiary responsibility (see Chapter 6), the trial of Osama bin Laden would be quite complicated in national courts, since many countries (USA, England and France, among others) would claim that they have jurisdiction on the crimes committed by bin Laden or Al Qaida in their territories (competence *ratione loci*), and against their citizens (competence *ratione personae*)), that is, terrorism and/or crimes against humanity. But the US response to terrorism in previous cases, with allegations of torture and inhumane treatment, may have made him take the decision to resist from arrest.

The bin Laden case was valid and justifiable from the IHL framework, but it is far from the ideal long term solution to international terrorism, that must be sought if a country desires to fight the root causes of terrorism, and preventing terrorist groups from recruiting new members and demoralizing their leaders.

A solely military response to terrorism may bring a short-term solution, but it creates long-term problems, and the threat may be dormant, waiting for an opportunity to rise again. Also, the State shall not use illegal methods of warfare to fight combatants, even when they use perfidy or other forbidden instruments against him.

A comprehensive response to terrorism must include:

- The gathering of intelligence (The operation of gathering intelligence (from the enemy) is different than gathering proof in inquiries for criminal instruction (against the citizen). In IHL, there is no need for a judicial warrant to gather intelligence from the enemy, because it is within the executive power of any military operation) with legal methods (in International Humanitarian Law, the proper legal framework applicable), so they can be used in court for a fair trial;

- An International or Internationalized Criminal Court, competent to prosecute and punish for crimes in international law, like terrorism;

- An executive organ to comply its judicial mandates, including arrest, detention, intimations and notifications, which can be a Peacekeeping Operation. Example: the functions and authority given to the United Nations Transitional Administration in East Timor (UNTAET) and United Nations Mission in Kosovo (UNMIK).

- The respect of the dignity of the human being, in all cases and at all times.

There is no need for specific laws and regulations to fight terror. The Geneva Conventions, especially Common Article 3, does not undermine the counterterrorism effort. These Conventions were created right after World War II. They were aware of the military needs as much as the humanitarian protection, and abuses that could happen when these regulations are not respected.

Humanitarian law and human rights were not created in time of peace and political stability. On the contrary, their *raison d'être* was to create a legal framework to respond effectively to most serious crises. Human rights are not superfluous, and cannot be ignored in harsh times, even when some of them may be suspended in cases of emergency. On the contrary, it is the ground for an effective response to threats against international peace and security.

The transition to peace in countries ravaged by armed conflicts characterized by the use of terrorism and other illegal methods of warfare shall be made with full compliance of human rights, such as:

- An independent ombudsman or other channel for complaining with enough legal enforcement to examine complaints from civilians against police or military officers;

- Monitor the police and military force from recruitment requirements to everyday bureaucratic activities, and assure participation of the entire population in the recruitment;

- Disciplinary regulations, human rights training and codes of conduct;

- Recording interrogations and hearings, allowing a lawyer to be present when the person is accused of crimes, in National or International Law;

- Promulgate national laws according to international human rights legal framework;

- National laws promoting equality and affirmative action to minorities;

- Fair, fast and accessible judicial and prosecution systems;

- Creation of executive agencies to promote equality and human rights;

- Respect equality and human rights in all government policies, from economic fomentation to youth participation in debates of polemic law propositions.

In conclusion, we affirm that IHL is the core value for the maintenance of international peace and security, and for combating terrorism and other threats to the stability of a country (Human Rights are likely to be respected in States where the rule of law prevails, because there is a sustainable peace. However, if a State is so weak that it cannot maintain the rule of law for the benefit of its citizens, and peace is threatened, IHL is the set of rules that will guide the conduct of all operations against the spoilers of the peace process).

11. STATE SOVEREIGNTY: A SHIELD OR A TARGET?

The international cooperation between intelligence agencies and efforts by Governments, exposed in the previous Chapters, are not always smooth. The Pakistani Government, for instance, strongly disapproved the operation carried out in Pakistan, without its knowledge or consent, by the United States Special Forces in May 2011, which resulted in the death of Osama Bin Laden (ABC News, May 02, 2011, <www.abcnews.go.com>).

Islamabad declared that operation Geronimo carried out in May 2011 in a walled compound to kill or capture the man sought for a decade for terrorist acts and support to terrorist groups, is a clear violation of its territory and sovereignty. There were also complaints about attacks using drones and other actions without previous communication.

In July 2011, the US Congress received the information that Osama Bin Laden lived a long time in Abbottabad, near the main Pakistani Military Academy, and resolved to suspend a military aid of US$ 800 million to Pakistan. Tensions also arose after Admiral Mike Mullen declared that Pakistanese security forces have killed the journalist Syed Saleem Shahzad, after he published that extremist persons had been recruited by the Pakistan Army (RESENHA, Jul 10, 2011, <www.exercito.gov.br>).

The relations between countries, as stated in the UN Charter, Article 2, are founded in the Principle of Equal Sovereignty of States, in order to maintain international peace and security, develop friendly relations among countries, cooperate in international level to solve economic, social, intellectual or humanitarian problems, and harmonize the efforts of nations towards common ends.

Nevertheless, certain actors of contemporaneous warfare are not bound to UN Principles, for example in Asymmetrical conflicts, where one or more parties are not recognized as international legal persons (rebels, militia, revolutionaries, dissident soldiers, guerilla, liberation fighters) where there is no clear front, with territories that are totally controlled by one of the parties, and combatants engage in conflict with no compliance with, or even knowledge of, International Humanitarian Law or Law of Armed Conflicts.

In Asymmetrical Warfare, the parties are not equal in structure, strength, logistics, methods and technology. In Non International Armed Conflicts, the disproportionality is caused by military resources available only to States, mainly the financial support of taxes paid by its citizens.

Nowadays other warring actors are available in the theater of operations, like warlords, drug traffickers, criminal organizations and terrorist groups, or a mixture of them (Ex: guerilleros that have also become drug traffickers in order to maintain their operations, and criminal organizations may use terror to gain the attention of the media). All these groups have economic achievement when operating in a feeble State, because they spend less money in bribes, security and disguising.

Since there is no front, nor international legal persons in both sides, the Asymmetrical Warfare may be conducted in more than one country, and they may be opposing the party or supporting it, creating an Internationalized Armed Conflict, very easy to be found, and very difficult to be proved.

The Asymmetrical Warfare is mainly the use of means and strategies of combat in order to explore their qualities (Positive Asymmetry) or the weaknesses of the enemy (Negative Asymmetry) (GRANGE, David. Asymmetric Warfare: Old Method, New Concern. <blackboard.jfsc.ndu.edu>). But the main difference between the parties is the speed in battle.

The strong and more capable party in a Conflict wants a quick victory, because the maintenance of a high technology war structure is very expensive, and a prolonged war may become unpopular among their citizens. The weaker party, on the contrary, gains with a slow combat. By detecting the mistakes of the enemy and attacking specific points, they cause demoralization and win with less combat capability.

Non-State actors, not by coincidence, usually choose to carry their operations in unfavorable terrain and conditions (jungle, mountain and desert are the favorite ones) in order to slow conventional State troops and make their support more expensive. Also, they attack new and inexperienced troops and by surprise (through ambushes and sabotages).

It has already been exposed that Guerrilla Warfare is a legal method of combat in IHL. Besides, if a group does not have, or does not want to use, a dialogue channel or by any other means a political participation in that country, it is reasonable that they take in arms to oppose the Government.

The illicit conduct arises for non State actors, like terrorists, concerning both the *jus ad bellum* and the *jus in bello*, in the cases exemplified below.

When a terrorist makes known he has religious, ideological or moral reasons to hold weapons against the government, he implicitly affirms that he is beyond International Humanitarian Law. Thus, he believes he does not need to obey IHL rules, because his objectives are too important for them to be limited, even by humanitarian principles. The *jus ad bellum* used to fight is unsustainable, no matter against whom.

About *jus in bello*, when they take up arms in an urban environment, among the civilian population, they are taking shelter within Protected Persons in the Law of Armed Conflicts. This conduct is considered a Perfidy, and may be considered a Crime in International Law. Other examples of Perfidy commonly committed in modern warfare are the kidnappings and assassination of members of sanitary services, humanitarian relief organizations and journalists.

The terrorist warfare is even more devious, because they do not just disguise among the civilian population, but they also attack sensitive targets of this population, causing widespread terror with the purpose to decrease the police power of the government, which makes the citizens oppose the government.

The police power is an important part of the sovereignty of a State, necessary to enforce law and order by legal sanctions, inducements, physical means and coercion, in order to guarantee the health and safety of their citizens.

In other words, diminishing the police power is an attempt against the sovereignty of a Nation, so the terrorist attack is a blow to the existence of a Nation, and a crime in International Law, as exposed previously.

When a country has terrorists (or other non State actors in international law) on its territory, acting outside the rules of International Humanitarian Law, and they are able to conduct their operations, there are two possibilities: the State is supporting the terrorist group, or is unable to deal with it.

In both cases, the international community must intervene when the State cannot deal with the terrorists alone, in order to restore and maintain the sovereignty of the Nation, and protect the civilian population. In these cases, it is unlikely that diplomacy will work, because the groups won't dialogue, and there is no viable negotiation when the group has economic and logistical advantages by maintaining a fragile State as a cover for their operations.

When the situation reaches this level, a Peace Operation is an available solution to the international community to react against this menace to international peace and security, and restore and preserve a safe and secure environment for the civilian population.

The Pakistani government may not support Al Qa'ida actively, but the terrorist group was taking advantage from their sovereignty as a shield to carry on their operations, and the targets were many Nations of the West (The United States, France and England, for example).

The Washington-Islamabad tension in 2011 could have been solved much easily if the international community and Pakistan considered terrorism a crime in international law, and al Qa'ida a non-State player acting outside IHL in terms of objective (*jus ad bellum*) and methods (*jus in bello*). From this point of view, the incursion in Pakistani territory is completely genuine, and the intention of US troops was not to occupy or raid foreign territory, but to find and neutralize a combatant, and a person sought for crimes in international law.

This case shows the need that a peacekeeping force needs soldiers trained specifically for this kind of operation, in order to provide a counterterrorism capability available to deal with potential spoilers of the peace process. If Blue Helmets have the legitimacy, they must also have the equipment and training to deal with persons not willing to dialogue or negotiate.

We conclude that State's Sovereignty can not just be a shield for terrorist activities but also the main target of terror. And in both cases, a Peacekeeping Mission is a solution to the terrorist menace in fragile countries, as well as other menaces to peace and security.

CONCLUSION

The main sources of international humanitarian law are consuetudinary, but there are also the Hague Regulations of 1907, about the laws and customs of war on Land, the Geneva Conventions of 1949, the two Additional Protocols of 1977, and many other conventions restraining and/or prohibiting certain weapons. These regulations shall apply to all persons engaged in combat, no matter what kind of combatant s/he is, or the compliance to its rules.

Additionally, in any circumstances an armed conflict is regulated by Article 3 Common to the Four Geneva Conventions of 1949. In this respect, the International Court of Justice has considered it the least considerations of humanity, a regulation applicable to armed conflicts, be they international or not.

As previously exposed, in all kinds of armed conflict, one of the most important rules for the conduct of hostilities is that all parties do the distinction between themselves, as warring parties, and persons not directly involved in the conflict, like the civilian population, armed groups that surrendered or become *hors de combat*, by illness, injuries, detention or other causes.

Also, all persons that are not, or no longer, participating in the conflict shall be treated humanely, and they shall not suffer acts against their lives and physical integrity, including mutilations, torture or other cruel treatments. In addition, any person engaged in combat, disregarding his nationality, must respect the core rules for the conduct of hostilities, be they armed forces, militia, criminal organizations or terrorists.

However, the asymmetry of a conflict, especially in technological resources, may lead the defavorized party to disrespect IHL rules, in order to endure in action, that is, take the only possible alternative to keep fighting. Nonetheless, this option is illegal, and must be considered a crime in international law. In legal terms, this is how terrorism arises.

Thus, in order to prevent terror, the international community must show that it is not a legal option to any party in a conflict, and confirm it in both strategic and tactical levels.

The best way for the combatant to survive is to avoid the enemy to locate him and identify the enemy troops in the field. This disguise can be done by many legal methods (camouflages, *ruses de guerre*, counterintelligence, etc.).

On the other hand, if one combatant tries to disguise himself among the civilian population, by wearing civilian clothes during the attack, or using the proximity of civilian persons or property to shield themselves, to benefit from the statute of protected person, they are not only disguising themselves, but are also exposing the civilian population to the danger of collateral damage. This is Perfidy, and is considered a crime in international law.

Terrorists go further. They do not only use Perfidy to carry on their operations, covering themselves as non-combatants, but they also target Protected Persons or Properties, with the intent to spoil the sovereignty of a State. By doing this, they put in danger the same State that protects the civilian population. This is a crime against humanity, and in this way the violators of LoAC and IHL must be prosecuted for crimes of international nature.

Today slavery and pirating are considered crimes of international character, but a few centuries ago the efforts against these two illegal conducts were not considered as such. Until the international community became aware that slavery and pirating must be fought worldwide, their perpetrators still had safe havens to carry on their businesses.

During the Eighteenth Century many international agreements were signed to restrain slavery. Some of them were successful, and many were not, due to the absence of proper institutions and procedures for enforcement. The first international document specifically related to slavery was the 1815 Declaration relative to the Universal Abolition of Slave Trade, with limited scope and applicability.

Due to a doctrinary evolution, now slavery is considered:

- A crime in international law, regardless of any quality of the person (race, sex, etc.);

- When committed by a government, it is a crime against humanity;

- If committed by a nation at war against the citizens of the opponent, a war crime.

Piracy is similar to an act of aggression, but committed by non-State actors against a vessel. They are not mere acts of robbery and violence, but an act of interference to free trade among nations, and a menace to international commerce. If the international community did not consider pirating a crime in international law, the efforts to fight pirates would be palliative.

Terrorism is the worldwide hazard of the XXIst Century, as slavery and pirating were in the past. Appropriate understanding of the criminal act is a must to do a suitable countering, and it is reasonable to believe that terrorism will follow the same path as the previous international menaces.

In the past, threats to international peace and security were dealt by each country separately, according to their military capability and their financial possibilities. However, nowadays a Peace Operation is an instrument capable of fighting these menaces in countries that don't have enough resources to deal with it (fragile countries), because it may bring legitimacy and unity of effort for all those who deal with perils to peace.

Terrorism is a threat to the State Sovereignty, and therefore to the existence of a Nation. Be it small or huge, be the victim a strong or failing State, it shall be considered a threat to international peace and security, and a crime in international law, to be fought adequately both in tactical and strategic levels.

In conclusion, fighting terror is the challenge for the international community in this century. Peace Operations capable of countering terrorism, authorized by their mandate and their Rules of Engagement, and also authorized to act as the executive organ of International Criminal Tribunals, together with proper doctrine of terrorism as a crime in international law, and intelligence services to collect evidence according to International Humanitarian Law, are a great opportunity to have a long-standing counter terrorism policy.

BIBLIOGRAPHY

ABC News, Available at <www.abcnews.go.com>. Accessed in May 02, 2011.

BALMOND, Louis. *Droit du recours à la force*. Université de Nice, 2010.

BBC News. Available at <news.bbc.co.uk>. Accessed in May 02, 2011.

BOLZ, Frank Jr; DUDONIS, Kenneth J. *Counterterrorism Handbook*. CRC, 2002

BOUCHET-SAULNIER, Françoise. *La Guerre contre le terrorisme et le droit humanitaire*. Université de Nice, 2010.

BOUVIER, Antoine A. *International Humanitarian Law and the Law of Armed Conflict*. Peace Operations Training Institute, 2008.

BROWNLIE, Ian. *Principles of Public International Law*. Oxford Press, 2008.

CONOIR, Yvan. *The Conduct of Humanitarian Relief Operations: Principles of Intervention and Management*. Peace Operations Training Institute, 2008.

FOLHA ONLINE, Available at < http://www1.folha.uol.com.br/folha/reuters/> Access in: Jun 12 2011.

GASSER, Hans Peter. *Acts of Terror, Terrorism and International Humanitarian Law*, Université de Nice, 2010.

HÅRLEMAN, Christian. *An Introduction to the UN System: Orientation for Serving on a UN Field Mission*. Peace Operations Training Institute, 2008.

JONES, Bruce. *Looking to the Future: Peace Operations in 2015*, Recueil de Lectures du Séminaire d'approfondissement des Missions de Paix de Nations Unies. UQAM, 2011.

MARIGHELLA, Carlos. *Minimanual do Guerrilheiro Urbano*, New World Liberation Front, 1970, p. 32.

MEDHURST, Paul. *Global Terrorism*. Peace Operations Training Institute, 2008.

MEYROWITZ, Henri. *Le principe de l'egalité des belligérants devant le droit de la guerre*. Université de Nice, 2010.

MILLET-DEVALLE, Anne-Sophie. *Religions et Droit International Humanitaire*. Université de Nice, 2010.

SECONDAT, Charles de (Baron de Montesquieu). *L'esprit des lois*. Université de Nice, 2010.

MOULIER, Isabelle. *La répression des crimes de Droit International*. Université de Nice, 2010.

PICTET, Jean. *Les principes du Droit International Humanitaire*. Université de Nice, 2010.

PROGRAMME HUMANMED. *Guerre Asymétrique et droit international humanitaire, possibilités de développement*. Université de Nice, 2010.

RAM, Sunil. *The History of United Nations Peacekeeping Operations During the Cold War: from 1945 to 1987*. Peace Operations Training Institute, 2008.

RAM, Sunil. *The History of United Nations Peacekeeping Operations Following the Cold War: from 1988 to 1996*. Peace Operations Training Institute, 2008.

RAM, Sunil. *The History of United Nations Peacekeeping Operations From Retrenchment to Resurgence: 1997 to 2006*. Peace Operations Training Institute, 2008.

REPORT OF THE INTERNATIONAL COMMISSION OF JURISTS, *Assessing Damage, Urging Action*. Report of the Eminent Jurists Panel on Terrorism, Counter-Terrorism and Human Rights. Université de Nice, 2008, pg. 83.

RESENHA ONLINE. Available at <www.exercito.gov.br>. Accessed July 10, 2011.

RONA, Gabor. *Interesting Times for International Humanitarian Law: Challenges from the War on Terror*. Université de Nice, 2010.

ROTH, Kenneth. *The Law of War in the War on Terror.* Université de Nice, 2010.

ROUSSEAU, Jean-Jacques. *Du Contrat Social.* Université de Nice, 2010.

SOBEL, Lester A. *Political Terrorism,* Facts on File, New York, 1978.

UNITED NATIONS. Security Council Resolutions and other UN documents. Available at <www.un.org>. Access June 10th 2010.

VEUTHEY, Michel. *Cours de Droit International Humanitaire.* Université de Nice, 2010.

VEUTHEY, Michel. *Perspectives et propositions pour mieux faire respecter le droit international humanitaire.* Université de Nice, 2010.

WILKERSON, Philip R., RINALDO, Richard J. *Principles for the Conduct of Peace Support Operations.* Peace Operations Training Institute, 2008.

###

This book is the opinion of the author, and nothing else; it does not represent the opinion of any government, organization or any third parties.
Also, it does not have any sensitive or confidential information. I always play by the rules.

Thank you for your interest in reading this ebook. I really appreciated that.

Certainly many people will not agree with it, as it's common in any Law discussion... So I would like to know your point of view.

Feel free to send suggestions, comments and opinions to rogeriocietto@uol.com.br, subject Combating the Good Combat. Your email is very welcome.

I regret to inform that you will not find me on Facebook, Twitter, Orkut or any related media.

Few information about me:

Academic Formation

1998 - 2002 – University Degree in Law.

Law College of Itu, Faditu, Brazil

2004 - 2005 - Post-Graduation in Tributary Law.
Law College of Itu, Faditu, Brazil
2008 - 2008 - Post-Graduation in Complementary Applications to Military Sciences - Law.
Army Administration School, EsAEx, Salvador, Brazil
2009 - 2010 - Post-Graduation (Specialization) in International Humanitarian Law
HUMANMED Program - Université de Nice, France
2011 - 2012 - Professional Qualification in Peace Operations
Peace Operations Training Institute, United States of America
Military Organizations I have been:
2008 - Army Administration School, Salvador, Brazil

2009 - 8th Military Region, Amazon Rainforest, Belém, Brazil

2010 - Amapá Border Company, Oiapoque, Brazil

2011 - Department of Engineering and Construction, Brasília, Brazil

2012 - Brazilian Battalion in Haiti, Port-au-Prince, Haiti

2013 – Special Operations Command, Goiânia, Brazil